THE REAL U

THE REAL U

Building Brands That Resonate with Students, Faculty, Staff, and Donors

ROBERT M. MOORE

WASHINGTON, D.C.

Council for Advancement and Support of Education (CASE).
Education's leading resource for knowledge, standards, advocacy, and training in alumni relations, communications, fundraising, marketing, and related activities.

Library of Congress Cataloging-in-Publication Data

Moore, Robert M. (Robert Mitchell), 1948-
  The real u : building brands that resonate with students, faculty, staff, and donors / by Robert M. Moore.
     p. cm.
  Other title: Real you
  Includes bibliographical references and index.
  ISBN 978-0-89964-424-0 (pbk.)
  1. Education, Higher--Marketing--Case studies. 2. Branding (Marketing)--
Case studies. 3. Universities and colleges--Case studies. I. Title. II. Title: Real you.

  LB2342.82.R425 2010
  378.068'8--dc22

                                                            2010002904

Book design: O2 Collaborative Inc.
Art Director: Angela Carpenter Gildner
Editorial Director: Julie K. Schorfheide

COUNCIL FOR ADVANCEMENT AND
SUPPORT OF EDUCATION
1307 New York Avenue, NW
Suite 1000
Washington, DC 20005-4701
www.case.org

CASE EUROPE
3rd Floor, Paxton House
30 Artillery Lane
London E1 7LS
United Kingdom

CASE ASIA-PACIFIC
Unit 05-03
Shaw Foundation Alumni House
11 Kent Ridge Drive
Singapore 119244

CONTENTS

ACKNOWLEDGMENTS

MANY PEOPLE ARE RESPONSIBLE for the book you hold in your hands today. Credit (or blame) should go to them. First, the remarkable staff at CASE—principally Julie Schorfheide, Lori Woehrle, Liz Reilly, and Rae Goldsmith—who have encouraged me both in this endeavor and in other work with the organization. Next, my colleagues at Lipman Hearne, who have been patient with me while I kept my head buried in the manuscript. Notably, Beth Drews, Joselyn Zivin, Libby Morse, Ken G. Kabira, Elizabeth Berry, and Sara Stern, who have pushed my thinking about branding principles in the higher ed setting—and my partners (Tom Abrahamson, Rodney Ferguson, Greg Larkin, Donna Van De Water, and Tim Westerbeck), who gave me permission to do this work. I have also learned a lot from a long list of people whose organizations I've been privileged to serve, including John Haeger, Fred Hurst, and M. J. McMahon at Northern Arizona University; Marc Raney and Sharon Jones Schweitzer at Trinity University; Jack Shannon and Lisa Grider (late of Seton Hall University); Bob Harty (late of Georgia Tech); Joyce Muller of McDaniel College; Susan Shullaw of the University of Iowa; Nancy Davis of University of North Carolina at Chapel Hill; Sergio Gonzalez and Jackie Menendez of the University of Miami; Jerry Lewis of the University of Texas at Arlington; Jim Moore of the University of Arizona Foundation; and Michael Spence, Marian Theobald, and Jas Chambers of the University of Sydney. This list would also be far more incomplete without mention of Dave McKinney of the University of Idaho and the University of New Mexico, who got me started in this business; Martin Grenzebach and John Glier of GrenzebachGlier and Associates, who deepened my understanding of development work; and Bob Lipman and Nancy Levner, founding partners of Lipman Hearne, who took a chance on me.

To Andy Goodman I owe the title, and to the Moore clan (Marilyn, Dorothy, and Andy), unending, reciprocal devotion.

INTRODUCTION

GREAT BRANDS ARE BUILT ON GREAT EXPERIENCES. All stakeholders—students or faculty members, administrators or alumni—have earned a unique brand perception based on how they believe they were or are treated by the institution, how they believe the promise you made to them was or was not kept. Each prospect—an inquiring student, the finalist in a faculty search, an alumnus or donor asked to become part of a new initiative—has a set of fundamental beliefs about your institution, based on a complex set of inputs that create an expectation of the experience that the individual will have. Some of these inputs are deliberate and purposeful—the marketing messages that you project, the direct conversations that you have—and some derive from elements that are less in your control: the weather on the day the prospect takes a campus tour, a blowhard at a cocktail party talking about your institution in terms that would make you grimace, a job seeker whose responses in an interview either elevate or degrade your reputation for producing quality graduates.

Brands are based in who you really are—the Real U. No amount of glossy brochures, boastful speeches, Flash-driven Web sites, or eye-catching advertising can make up for a poorly designed or inadequately delivered experience. Great promotion of a bad product only accelerates its demise. Guy Kawasaki, the former chief marketing officer at Apple, offers the first rule of marketing: "Get better reality."[1] When the Real U is strong, not only can your brand promise be made, it can be fulfilled.

Great brands resonate in the mind. They set up an echo chamber in which the brand promise reverberates with the needs and expectations that people hold for the brand. And a well-managed brand combines brand messaging and lived reality that, handled correctly, becomes powerfully defining for the individual, the group, and the institution.

Nowhere is this more true than in education, a field in which you make a promise—to students, their parents, the community—that you will deliver a certain kind of experience and that the experience will have lasting value. Parents are handing their children to you in hopes that they will come back happy, smarter, and ready for anything. Young people are trusting you with their future. Adult students are counting on you to provide the kind of training and perspective that will enable them to achieve the next stage of their dreams. Alumni want to wear your brand proudly as they sweat on the treadmill trying to lose a few pounds. Employers are banking on you. The community expects you to live up to your town/gown pledge. Your brand has meaning—*life* meaning—in ways that far outstrip brand affiliation or attachment in the consumer products arena.

You want proof? In a word: Harvard.

Harvard is in your head—and everyone else's. More precisely, the Harvard brand and all it stands for is securely lodged in your cranial nooks and crannies, living there as the measure of all things great and powerful in academe. You might not like some of the things Harvard stands for, you might be envious of the reverberations that Harvard sets up in your head, you might wish that you or yours could wear that Harvard hoodie honestly, but there's no doubt that those reverberations are there. But why?

Common wisdom has it that academic reputations are made up of three factors: age, size, and endowment. While Harvard's 1636 founding makes it "first in class" in the United States, Oxford holds the crown in the English-speaking world. Size-wise, Harvard's enrollment is far below that of major public universities such as Ohio State University or the University of Michigan. But in academe—as in other areas—a lot depends on what you're measuring. With 15 million volumes, Harvard's library is the largest academic library in the United States; Harvard's range of programs (particularly in the post-baccalaureate arena) is second to none, and its ability to "punch above its weight" in terms of influential graduates (including 18 percent of U.S. presidents) enables it to cast a long shadow. And in endowment—well, even in the economic maelstrom of late 2008, Harvard's endowment remained fully 50 percent higher than that of Yale, its closest "big bucks" competitor. These factors give Harvard the ability to maintain admit and yield percentages that are the envy of the sector, historic alumni giving rates outdone by only the Seven Sisters, a faculty chock-full of experts anointed by the national press, highly ranked professional programs, and a succession of successful "three-comma" fundraising campaigns—all of which reinforce and advance an unassailable brand.

Think about it. Lesser-known institutions don't generally fashion themselves the "Princeton on the Platte" or the "Amherst of the Adirondacks," but the attempt to seize brand value through (occasionally specious) linkage has gone global when it comes to Harvard. Consider these iterations, some of which are no longer in use:

- University of Nebraska Omaha: Harvard on the Prairie
- Catawba Valley Community College: Harvard on the Highway
- Moscow University: Harvard on the Hill
- Baylor University: Harvard on the Brazos
- Nicholls State University: Harvard on the Bayou

- Tsinghua University: Harvard on the Yangtze
- Lamar University: Harvard on the Neches
- University of Illinois at Chicago: Harvard on the Rocks

Harvard has undoubtedly earned its reputation. Say "Harvard" and a whole litany of associations springs to mind, their tint depending upon your attitude toward well-funded elites. But for those institutions that don't have an eleven-figure endowment, nearly 400 years of history, top-rank programs, or a name whose inclusion on a c.v. clearly signals a job applicant's potential, does brand matter? And, more important, can it be enhanced?

The answers? Yes. And yes. And this book will teach you how.

And when it comes to why ...

PRESSURE FROM ALL SIDES

The pressures on higher education institutions are intense, and growing. In Australia, the Rudd government proposed a new higher education funding scheme as soon as it took office in 2007, one that emphasizes outcomes of education and allows for greater differentiation among the national and regional institutions. In the U.K., the Brown government's ambitious access agenda ran into the stark budget reality of the 2008–2009 global recession and had to simultaneously freeze the levels of grants to students while tuition crept upward. In Asia, the National University of Singapore remains an "enterprise" investment of the national government, but recessionary forces and budget realities have limited the institution's ability to achieve its plans for global prominence. Only in the Gulf States, where plentiful oil revenue combines with a growing understanding of the importance of a well-educated populace, does the higher education sector find itself in rapid ascent, with campuses and international collaborations becoming commonplace in Doha, Dubai, and Riyadh.

In the United States, the clamor for greater accountability, tuition controls, increased access, and better outcomes continues to rise in the elected sector. State legislators simultaneously reduce their historic contribution to the educational enterprise and put caps on tuition. The federal government layers on increased regulations and continues to squeeze the buying power of Pell grants.[2]

Everywhere, prospective students want a fully interactive introduction to the institution, a warm Web community that welcomes them before they arrive; an assurance that they will fit in, have fun, gain friends, get lucky, and—oh, yes—learn something useful at their school of choice. And did I mention they'd prefer not to pay very much?

Current students want everything from high-intensity seminars taught by full professors to high-flow showerheads in the residence halls, four-star cuisine in the dining hall, an exciting off-campus life—often including a semester or year abroad—and a career services department that puts them on the fast track toward fulfilling their professional dreams.

Parents want to know that their children will be safe, that their investment is worth it, that after commencement the proud degree-holder will not be sitting on the couch eating Cheetos and watching Oprah, and that the "My child and my money go to Old Great U" bumper sticker stands as a lasting badge of pride, not an admission of mediocrity.

Alumni want their friends, neighbors, and employers to nod respectfully when they hear the name of alma mater—or at least to have heard of it—and want to maintain an idealized image of both their college years and their institution. They don't want to hear that it needs money, is eroding in stature or capacity, or is unable to either (a) recruit the students who will raise the institutional profile or (b) admit their kids as legacies even if those same kids would dramatically fatten the lower end of the bell curve.

Trustees want higher rankings, balanced budgets, and winning teams.

Faculty members want greater respect, a continued role in governance, and more pay.

Adjuncts and TAs want union protections.

And we humble marketing folks? Hey, we just want a realistic budget to raise awareness and increase understanding of the institution we serve.

BRAND ADVANTAGES

The advantages of a strong, focused, and valued brand are hard to overstate. In the commercial world, brand value is readily calculated: If Coca-Cola or McDonald's suddenly decided to go out of business, cash out its hard assets (inventory, factories, bottling plants, patty-making machinery, etc.) and kill off its product lines, the difference between its fire sale income and its current market capitalization is the value of the brand. As an equation:

$$Brand\ value = market\ capitalization - asset\ value$$

And that's not even new math.

In higher education, brand value is harder to calculate, though no less real. A strong academic brand can help stimulate inquiries and applications, improve yield, lower the discount rate, increase alumni pride and support, provide a reputational context for grant applications and research proposals, provide legislative cover, increase the effectiveness of advocacy efforts, generate media interest, reassure and encourage volunteer leadership, aid in faculty recruitment, and enhance student retention and graduation rates.

Strong brands are magnetic: They attract adherents.

Strong brands are directional: They focus attention toward a specific mission or purpose and invite engagement with that mission.

Strong brands are enlightening: They illuminate key aspects of a college or university and create, through an intellectual chiaroscuro, a clear and dimensional portrait of the institution.

Strong brands are motivating: They encourage or compel action.

But what the heck are they?

BRAND AS STORY

There are as many definitions of *brand* as there are brand experts, each of whom feels compelled to derive his or her singular definition. In the mind of the beholder, though, a brand is simply a believable and compelling narrative.

Why brand as narrative? Because stories touch something deep in our lives, going back to the days when we hunkered around that communal fire recounting and repeating the overlapping threads of narrative that defined us as a family, a tribe, a people.

In his book *The End of Marketing as We Know It*, Sergio Zyman talks about the core mistake that Coca-Cola made when it introduced New Coke: The popularity of the drink that came to be known as Coke Classic wasn't in its taste, which consistently came up behind Pepsi in blind tastings, but in its story. "We buy Coke for the totality of the product, and that includes the fact that it's old and familiar and we feel comfortable with it."[3] People knew where Coke fit in their lives; they were passionately attached to what it symbolized, how it connected—not necessarily how it tasted. They knew how it related to their own personal narrative, to the picture they had of themselves. And in that picture, the constancy or stability of Coke, as opposed to the youth and dynamism of Pepsi, was a key element. A guerrilla response to New Coke, fueled by news feeds and early viral word-of-mouth, knocked it out of the picture, and Coke sales went through the roof.

When you think of another iconic brand, Volvo, it's not just the word safety that pops into mind but the stories that Volvo owners tell about the beer truck that veered across the centerline and smashed into them—and the carful of folks who limped away from the wreck, shaken but alive. These owners might be your neighbors, family members, or friends, or they might be the solemn faces staring at you from a Volvo ad. No matter: If you're buying a car and safety is one of your primary concerns, you will no doubt think of Volvo, even if you end up buying a Hummer.

So what are the powerful brand stories in higher education? There are many.

The little engine that could: Gonzaga, Claremont College, Smith

The aristocrat: Harvard, Oxford, Yale, Cambridge, Notre Dame

The road less traveled: New School, Oberlin, UCSC, Reed, Open University

The Brand! New! Model: University of Phoenix, ASU

The captain and the cheerleader: Michigan, OSU, Florida

The arriviste: Duke, Wash U

While you might argue about some of these category titles or wish to add others to the list, my bet is that with each name—Phoenix or Duke or OSU—you had an instant snap of recognition, an inkling of the institution's story, that told you "I see why this is here" or "I think this should be in a different place." That response in itself proves the point: Each of these institutions has a brand story, and that story starts to tell us a lot about the place.

In this book, you'll learn how to understand your brand story; shape it to meet the interests, values, and needs of your stakeholders; and project it into the marketplace in powerful, compelling, and effective ways.

And the story starts, as many do: Once upon a time ...

_____

1. Harry Beckwith, *Selling the Invisible: A Field Guide to Modern Marketing* (New York: Warner Books, 1997), 3.

2. Texas Guaranteed Student Loan Corp., "The Value of the Federal Pell Grant Has Declined," *Edufacts*, April 2004, available at *Shoptalk Online* 255, May 18, 2004, *www.tgslc.org/shoptalk/2004/st255/st25504.cfm*.

3. Sergio Zyman, *The End of Marketing as We Know It* (New York: HarperBusiness, 1999), 48.

CHAPTER 1

WHY AND WHEN

ONCE UPON A TIME, *brand* was not only a term foreign to college and university campuses, it was widely regarded as an invader, an antibody that must be immediately and emphatically rejected to protect the health of the institution. But by 2007, that situation had dramatically changed, with 97 percent of higher education respondents to a national survey reporting that the words *brand* and *branding* were part of their institutional lexicon.[1]

Institutions have many reasons to investigate and advance brand positioning:

- Faltering enrollment, both in quality and quantity
- Unsustainable discount rate
- Trustee unrest

To Our Offshore Readers

Much of this chapter focuses on U.S. demographic and economic factors. While these issues—other than those associated with nontraditional students and distance learning—might not be relevant to your situation, the basics of brand building and enhancement that are covered in the next chapters are perfectly adaptable to any educational institution. A June 2009 Moody's report carries the subtitle "Higher Education Is Countercyclical Stimulant to Economic Growth but Faces Capital Shortage." Key findings are:

- Universities are expected to experience some stress, but be more sheltered than other sectors from the effects of the global recession.
- Public university credit quality will likely be steadier than that of private universities.
- The university sector will, over the long term, seek more independent sources of funding to finance growth and expansion.

- Changing market conditions
- Inert alumni
- Upcoming capital campaign
- New leadership

Even without these specific factors, the higher education environment includes a number of issues that create the need and the climate for serious brand work on the part of all institutions: demographics, the rise of distance learning, and the revenue realities within which colleges and universities must operate.

A Plethora of Definitions

Brand has as many definitions as there are branding experts—each of whom feels compelled to create a new model for understanding a basic concept.

The definitions begin—as all good stories do—around the campfire as our squatting ancestors poked sticks into the coals and tried to figure out (over generations, mind you) how to spend less time foraging and more time goofing off. Once the men had the synaptical snap that "the women can farm!" a new paradigm was born, and as soon as the women realized that they were getting a bum deal, they ordered the men to "keep those animals out of the field." This led to garden plots, fences, the domestication of animals, and collective herding (OK, I'm making gross generalizations and compressing millennia of history into a paragraph—but you get the idea). And collective herding led to the need to identify whose animals were whose under the doctrine of *animus revertendi* (you can look it up).

The etymology: from Old English *byrnan*—to burn.

Common usage: "anything hot or burning." Related concepts: brandish (v.), firebrand (n.).

Wikipedia: "the process of burning a mark into stock animals with thick hides so as to identify ownership."

And, although some African American fraternities have reverted to the branding iron as a symbol of brotherhood, inclusion, and sacrifice, our understanding and use of brand has evolved to signify a whole class of actions that, essentially, establish the distinction of one organization, product, or service from another.

Webster defines it as "a class of goods identified as being the product of a single firm or manufacturer."[a]

The U.S. Patent and Trademark Office equates trademark and brand: "A trademark includes any word, name, symbol, or device, or any combination, used, or intended to be used, in commerce to identify and distinguish the goods of one manufacturer or seller from goods manufactured or sold by others, and to indicate the source of the goods. In short, a trademark is a brand name."[b]

"This meaning was consecrated when, in 1905, Congress passed trademark legislation. The brand legally became 'a name, term, or design—or combination of these elements that is intended to clearly identify and differentiate a seller's products from a competitor's products.'"[c]

Marketing maven Philip Kotler defines brand as "a name, term, sign, symbol, or design, or combination of these, intended to identify the goods or services of one seller or group of sellers and to differentiate them from those of competitors."[d]

The American Marketing Association runs parallel to Kotler: "a name, term, design, symbol, or any other feature that identifies one seller's goods or services as distinct from those of other sellers."[e]

David Ogilvy emphasizes "the intangible sum of a product's attributes: its name, packaging, and price, its history, its reputation, and the way it's advertised."[f]

James B. Twitchell defines brands as "commercialized gossip" that "create an aura of differentiation around a product that distinguishes it from all others. ... [T]he brand does not just tell the product's story ..., it determines the viewer's response."[g]

Another Northwestern University professor,

Tim Calkins, defines brand as "a set of associations linked to a name, mark, or symbol associated with a product or service," saying further that "branding is about making a certain promise to customers about delivering a fulfilling experience and a level of performance."[h]

Personally, I prefer this definition: "Your brand is a promise, delivered as a compelling narrative based on those aspects of your service that differentiate you from your competitors."[i]

a. Webster's Third New International Dictionary.
b. www.uspto.gov/faq/trademarks.jsp#DefineTrademark.
c. James B. Twitchell, Branded Nation: The Marketing of Megachurch, College Inc., and Museumworld (New York: Simon & Schuster, 2004), 18.
d. Philip Kotler, Marketing Management, 7th ed. (New York: Prentice Hall, 1991), 442.
e. www.marketingpower.com/_layouts/Dictionary.aspx?dLetter=B.
f. whatis.techtarget.com/definition/0,,sid9_gci211703,00.html.
g. Twitchell, Branded Nation, 20, 40.
h. Alice M. Tybout and Tim Calkins, Kellogg on Branding (Hoboken, NJ: John Wiley & Sons, 2005), 1, ix.
i. Robert M. Moore, The Real U, 9.

DEMOGRAPHICS: THE GOOD, THE BAD, THE SCARY

The Good

The good news about demographics has to do with inheritance. The United States is in the midst of a phenomenal wealth transfer, both from Greatest Generation parents to Boomer kids, and from grownup Boomers to their offspring. In 1999, Boston College's Paul Schervish finished grinding the numbers and came out with an astonishing result: By his calculations, the "American inheritance" that is due to be distributed over the first half of the 21st century totals some $41 trillion.[2] Subsequent market fluctuations have kicked that number around somewhat, but it's still a large stack of nickels.

Schervish further estimated that approximately $6 trillion of this transfer would go to charitable causes—an assertion that a subsequent Charles Schwab study argued should be reduced;[3] but even if 15 percent of this transfer goes to educational entities (an average that has held up for many years, according to Giving USA), then nearly $1 trillion in bequests and annuities may be making its way into college and university coffers over the next 50 years. And as U.S. Senator Mitch McConnell pointed out (in a different context), "If you started the day Jesus Christ was born and spent $1 million every day since then, you still wouldn't have spent $1 trillion"[4] by January 2009. So the $1 with 12 zeroes after it will cover a lot of endowed professorships.

But you can't just sit back and wait for yours to arrive. The competition for the philanthropic dollar is more intense than ever, and Schwab's research suggests that Boomers—

with less certainty about Social Security and greater anxiety about the balance between length of life and available assets—might not be as ready to give as were earlier generations.

And there's another core truth about the philanthropic market that must be taken into consideration: Big gifts go to successful institutions. This happens in part because those institutions have built strong and ongoing relationships with high-net-worth individuals, but also because those individuals feel reassured that the institution will be able to successfully manage their philanthropic investment and not be overwhelmed or knocked off course by it. Those institutions that have built a reputation for solidity, innovation, impact, seriousness of intent, and staying power are simply more attractive to major donors, even if their endowment is already well north of a billion dollars. So in philanthropy as in other market arenas: Brand matters.

But what if you're not anticipating a major capital campaign? What's the relationship between brand value and alumni engagement? Oregon State University's James H. McAlexander and Harold F. Koenig, along with University of Portland's John W. Schouten, dug into this question in a 2006 study.[5] Postulating the university as a "marketing institution that offers a broad range of products and services to an equally broad range of consumers through many outlets and service providers under the auspices of its brand," the authors develop a thesis of the "brand community as the product of social relationships among users of a brand ... who recognize their commonality and who share rituals, traditions, and a sense of responsibility toward the brand." McAlexander et al. studied a variety of relationships within this brand community construct, concluding that "consumer interaction[s] with a product or service ... [that] create favorable impressions of the brand ... provide opportunities for building the university brand community in synergistic ways." After fielding a quantitative study testing their hypotheses about brand engagement, the authors conclude that alumni "integration in a brand community in higher education can contribute to such valued behaviors as donations, college referrals, engagement in alumni groups, and participation in continuing education."[6]

Research at Lipman Hearne shows that donors who are more engaged—who feel they know more—give more.[7] But do they give more because they know more, or do they know more because their giving opens them up to more streams of communication? We do know that when they're asked more—particularly when a generous interactive element is included in institutional outreach—alumni participation and average gift both rise.[8]

The Bad

For institutions that have grown large and healthy over the past decades as they have taken advantage of the increased numbers of traditional-age students passing through their turnstiles: Watch out; good times are coming to an end. According to the National Center for Education Statistics, the actual number of public high school graduates grew by nearly 16 percent from 1996 to 2002, then continued to grow at a slightly slower rate from 2002 to 2008. The center projected, however, that the total number of graduates would drop by more than 3 percent from 2008 to 2014, then would begin to rise slowly after that.[9]

It's not about gross numbers, though. The NCES reports that some states and regions will show a significant net increase in high school graduates while others show an equally significant net decrease.[10] And though total enrollment in degree-granting institutions is expected to increase by 2016—because of a greater percentage of the population enrolling in college (63 percent of high school graduates went directly into college in 2002, compared to 52 percent in 1970[11])—there are embedded factors that must be considered.

Willingness to travel. In 2006, Lipman Hearne conducted a study of high-achieving high school students, all of whom had been accepted by three or more colleges or universities, to investigate how they decided where to enroll. It's our belief that the real recruitment battle is now in yield, rather than applications, since the latter is greatly influenced by the common application, ease of online filing, etc. We broke the sample into two groups: Solid Achievers (SAT 1150–1299) and Academic Stars (SAT 1300+). The Solid Achievers were much more likely to attend an institution within 500 miles of home, and they wanted to go to a school where their friends were also going. The Academic Stars were much more ready to venture farther, and what most interested them was the reputation of the specific program in which they were going to study and the opportunity to be given an intellectual jolt more challenging than they had heretofore experienced.[12]

Ethnicity and readiness. Historically, the majority of domestic students at the nation's colleges and universities have been white. Moreover, because of persistent issues with our K–12 system and continuing social inequities, those students were also often the best prepared to succeed at the college level. But beginning in 2008, the percentage of white high school graduates has begun to diminish more rapidly than the overall pool, with fewer and fewer of them projected to be present in the population past 2020. In fact, in 1994, white students constituted 65 percent of all high school graduates; in 2018, they will comprise 48 percent.[13] And in 2006, nearly 70 percent of college students were white.[14] See the dilemma?

The increase we start to see in 2014 is substantially made up of African American and Hispanic students[15]—the majority of the former from challenged urban school districts, and the majority of the latter from Mexican American families, who have historically been far less likely to continue on to college than students from other Hispanic backgrounds.[16] So those students around whom so many institutions have built their market profiles and financial models—the reasonably qualified, able-to-pay, family-encouraged graduates of good public school systems, no matter their other demographic attributes—are growing scarcer every day. And the students who are taking their place—and upon whom our future prosperity and social progress are based—will be more likely to need greater levels of remediation, financial aid, and academic counseling than today's colleges and universities are ready to provide.

The impact of this ethnic and economic divide will be particularly felt in a number of states that rank among those facing the most dramatic growth rates over the next decade. In Nevada, Arizona, and Texas, significant numbers of graduating and incoming students are first-generation Mexican Americans—and in Florida, Virginia, the Carolinas, and Georgia, the population growth is markedly African American.

As a society, we have the responsibility and the need to educate people from all ethnic and socioeconomic groups so they can fulfill their potential. As a sector, though, higher education is ill-prepared to successfully take up the challenges of academic remediation, poverty, and inequality that are inherent in these demographic realities.

Gender. There are more men than women ages 15–24 in the United States—21.2 million versus 20.6 million, according to a 2008 U.S. Census Bureau report. But nationally, the male/female ratio on campus skews 57 percent female, a shift from the nearly even splits of the 1970s. The discrepancy is particularly pronounced at the lower income levels, with a 40/60 male/female break among families earning less than $30,000, compared to a 49/51 break among families earning more than $70,000. Among low-income African American families, the split is even more pronounced at 36/64, and among Hispanic families, it's 39/61.

The implications of these trends are potentially staggering for the lives of the individuals who don't feel prepared or motivated to attain a college degree, for our colleges and universities, and for our society as a whole. According to the Census Bureau, a person who holds a bachelor's degree will earn, on average, about $2.5 million over 40 years, while those who hold associate's degrees will earn about $1.8 million; high school graduates will earn a total of $1.4 million, and people lacking a high school diploma total only $1.1 million in lifetime earnings. A master's degree ups the earnings average to $2.8 million, while a professional degree raises it even higher: $5.2 million.[17] Simple math means that the high school graduate earns an average of $35,000 per year (in constant dollars) over his or her working life, while an individual with a bachelor's degree averages $62,500 and one with a professional degree averages $130,000. Education is truly the steppingstone out of poverty, and the failures of our K–12 system and our inability to motivate underprivileged youth to strive for and believe they can attain a college degree create a vicious cycle of continuing loss of talent, socioeconomic stagnation, and personal despair.

The Scary

OK, I'm going to say it: the University of Phoenix.

Founded in 1976, the University of Phoenix has grown to be the largest higher education institution in the country, with an enrollment of more than 420,000 students in 2009. Now owned by the Apollo Group, the university reported revenue of $2.3 billion in 2007 through both its online course offerings and its nearly 200 sites nationwide. Accredited by the North Central Association of Colleges and Schools and other disciplinary agencies, the university offers a full array of associate, baccalaureate, master's, and doctoral degrees (the latter in more narrow specialty areas). And while many may argue the quality of its educational offerings, the market value of its degree, the structure of its curriculum, or its student/faculty ratio, every term hundreds of thousands of people lay their money on the table (or click on PayPal) to attain a Phoenix degree. And that's the marketplace speaking.

A great deal of Phoenix's success has been in its focus on education for working adults— a population that historically has been poorly served by the majority of brick-and-mortar institutions. The University of Phoenix saw a marketplace opportunity—a large and growing population of adult students whose educational needs and career goals were being poorly served by existing structures; and recognizing the power of the Internet, the university moved to take advantage of it.

And the University of Phoenix is smart as a whip when it comes to marketing. First, it identified core segments where it could build a base—notably, the military, where soldiers, sailors, Marines, or Guardsmen (and/or their trailing spouses) cannot be sure where they will be weeks or months in the future, so the ubiquity of the Phoenix offer is key. Within those segments, Phoenix identified the most necessary or popular courses those individuals would need: business education, teacher education and certification, allied health education. Then, the university invests heavily in marketing outreach. Nearly 40 percent of its budget is dedicated to creating visibility, generating interest, triggering phone calls or click-throughs, and converting applicants to enrollees.

Most recently, Phoenix purchased naming rights to the stadium where the NFL's Arizona Cardinals play football on Sundays (and where the Western Regionals of the 2009 NCAA men's basketball tournament were held), a masterstroke that further suggests to the market that the University of Phoenix is a far more conventional enterprise than it actually is. Who can't imagine a couple of guys sitting on the couch watching the 2008 Superbowl broadcast from "beautiful University of Phoenix Stadium" having this conversation:

"What's the record of the University of Phoenix team?"

"I dunno, but I think they had a pretty good season."

Soon we can expect them to name their team and start selling licensed apparel: the University of Phoenix Phantoms; the University of Phoenix Distributed Servers; the University of Phoenix Fighting Capitalists. I'd buy the T-shirt.

Another factor that must be taken into account under the "scary" banner is the downstream sustainability of the revenue model used by many colleges and universities. In 2009, Moody's Investors Service issued its first negative outlook for all sectors of higher education since the credit-rating agency started publishing higher education outlooks in the 1990s.[18] Specific issues include:

- Increasing pressure on tuition and financial aid, with declines in household income, investments, and home equity
- Broad impact of investment losses on operations and philanthropy
- Illiquidity of balance sheets, amplified by alternative investments
- Volatility in debt markets and debt structures

The report emphasizes that not all institutions face the same financial pressures: "private universities that are not highly selective and already compete directly with regional public universities may see a greater number of students choose to enroll in local four-year public institutions. For public universities, students may choose to enroll in community colleges for two years before transferring to a four year university."[19]

The financial concerns associated with the 2008 market meltdown exacerbated the issues that Moody's had highlighted only a year earlier:

1. Adapting to changing student demand and customer preferences
Shifting demographics; changes to the socioeconomic makeup of the student population; growing numbers of nontraditional students; new educational delivery methods; cyclical popularity of degree offerings; the challenge of new curricula

2. Determining appropriate pricing strategies and policies
Unsustainable level of tuition increases; state and national scrutiny; stagnant family income; volatility in household net worth; high family debt levels; rise of the community college sector

3. Improving governance and management
Sarbanes-Oxley; increasing competition; capital intensiveness; the "privatization" of public institutions; unwieldy board structures; ambitious presidents with strategic plans with significant negative financial and credit implications

4. Increasingly complex balance sheet management strategies
Increased risk to liquidity without appropriate investment and debt management staff

5. Enhancing operational management
Weak operational management; arcane budgeting models; inability to determine revenues and costs associated with departments and schools; weak operating cash flow management

6. Determining appropriate levels of operational and capital spending
Need for a fundamental strategic evaluation of spending priorities; danger of "keeping up with the Joneses"; need to develop a more market-niche strategy

7. Defining institutional mission
Better definition and articulation of institutional mission to attract students and donors and compete for government funding

8. Shifting governmental funding paradigms
Vulnerability to shifts in federal, state, and local spending levels and priorities; need to focus on educating the public in order to sustain government investment

9. Understanding implications of increasing wealth concentration
Wealth concentration begets wealth concentration; endowment growth and success of multi-billion-dollar campaigns; need for mission positioning and strategic spending programs

10. Responding to heightened demand for transparency, questions regarding not-for-profit status of the sector
Increasing calls for transparency by parents, students, government, alumni; need for improved public communications strategies to explain their value proposition[20]

Lessons from a Former P&G Brand Manager

An interview with Gary E. McCullough, president and CEO of Career Education Corporation

Gary E. McCullough assumed the top post at Career Education Corporation—an organization that enrolls more than 90,000 students at 75 campuses in four countries—in March 2007 after a successful career at Procter & Gamble, Wm. Wrigley Jr. Company, and Abbott Laboratories. A brand marketer by background, McCullough had no prior experience in higher education.

Q: What lessons were "transportable" from your consumer goods background to the education sector?

A: First, that product quality is always the most important thing. When I came into CEC, we were not as focused on quality as we should have been. People come to us because they want something very specific: professional advancement. We had lost sight of that because we were focused primarily on gaining more and more new students—not on serving those we have with the best possible programs. So my first task was to answer the question "How do we get back in the education business in a quality fashion?"

Q: What steps did you take to improve your performance?

A: We suffered from a lack of data—and the sophistication to analyze those data—that would support a point of view or give us the ability to develop a strategy about where we needed to go or what we had to do to get there. So we stepped back and did a lot of research: What do we know about our brands? Why are people attracted to them? What are their expectations? How well do we perform relative to those expectations? After we had a good understanding of the answers to those questions, we made some basic business decisions—creating an environment in which local leadership could run each school effectively while taking advantage of our scale. We moved from a model where the most important measurement was revenue generation in the

form of new enrollments to a more balanced scorecard [that was] focused on the delivery of quality services. "Promise makers, promise keepers" became the mantra and expectation for our staff.

Q: You had a real mix of brands in your portfolio—some very strong and others not so strong. What was your approach to strengthen your brands?

A: When I started, we had about 23 brands. That was just too many for a company of our size [revenue of $1.7 billion in 2008]. Our research showed that we had some very strong brands— Le Cordon Bleu, American InterContinental University, Colorado Technical University—and others that were less defined, less distinct. At some of our campuses, the push to gain more students had resulted in the launch of programs that [diluted] the brand—taking what had been a distinctive and valued market position and blurring it. So through sale of some institutions and consolidation of others, we've reduced it to 13 brands, with an eventual goal of getting down to about six. This was a page right out of the P&G handbook: Focus on fewer brands with better differentiation, then put your resources behind them.

Q: In higher ed, which model do you think is stronger: the branded house or the house of brands?

A: Undoubtedly, the branded house provides more leverage. The connections that people make with one of your offerings—a school or curriculum—can add value to other offerings. But CEC was created and grown using a different model—a house of brands. What I'm trying to do is take the complexity out of that, focus on the strongest brands, and build real value in them by providing the desired experience and outcomes for our students.

Q: **What advice would you give to your colleagues in the nonprofit sector?**

A: I'd like to be profound, but the real work doesn't lend itself to profound statements. It's about fundamental blocking and tackling. It's about understanding what you do really well and differentiating yourself from competitors in your market space. If all you have as a differentiator is price and price alone, you're going to lose—someone can always do it more cheaply. Running any education institution—whether it's a nonprofit or a for-profit—is a business, and nonprofits have to get serious about business. You can't keep raising prices and using those increases to cover inefficiencies in the business model. If they do, as long as my quality is good, I'll have pricing power. Today's economy needs a qualified, educated workforce—and we will produce it, either through the nonprofit providers or through the businesses that provide an equivalent quality of service. Our students and our communities are looking for outcomes—and that's what we must provide.

THE PATH LESS TRAVELED

For many years the majority of colleges and universities have focused on traditional students. It made sense: They were (relatively) easy to find, they took advantage of the full "offer" (not just classes, but residence life, sports affiliation, clubs and activities, career services, etc.), and they were more likely to become "good" (a.k.a. "giving") alumni. Furthermore, their scores and standing as entering first-year students were key to institutional rankings, as were their retention and graduation rates, and they tended to be relatively undemanding—moving into and through their baccalaureate experience with the expectations that had been inculcated in them during their K–12 experience: You go to class, you do the work, you get graded, and, generally, life revolves around school.

For the adult student, those presumptions fall apart. The typical nontraditional student is a working adult with a broad range of responsibilities. Fully 60 percent are 30 years of age or older, married, with children. The trend lines that are visible in the traditional student marketplace—increasing numbers of African American and Hispanic students, predominance of female students—are also apparent in the nontraditional market. Their family situation means that they are not as mobile as the traditional student coming straight out of high school, who often wants to get away from home for an experience unmediated by his or her parents. These folks *are* the parents; and much as they might like to get away from time to time, they can't just go off on a two- or four-year hiatus. So issues of convenience and, in many cases, cost come very much into play.

And the market is growing. From autumn 2005 to autumn 2006, the number of people taking courses online jumped 35 percent, totaling more than 3 million students.[21] Predominantly undergraduate, these students flock to business, education, and allied health curricula. The internal market—faculty—is also increasingly invested in the adult and online sector. More than 96 percent of the nation's largest institutions (15,000+ students) have some online offerings, and 60 percent have fully built-out online programs. At doctoral and comprehensive institutions, more than 60 percent of faculty agree with the statement "Online education is critical to the long-term strategy of my institution."[22]

Simply put, adult students are the fastest growing sector of the market, with the ability to make up for the downturn in the supply of traditional students over the next decade. But they are not going to flock like sheep to the "standard" offer; institutions will have to in many cases reconfigure themselves to serve the needs and meet the expectations of these more mature students. And they will have to position themselves in the market as *the best solution* to the very real and very serious issues these adult learners are facing.

Does brand matter to these students? Absolutely, unequivocally, yes. Our direct, proprietary research at institutions around the country shows that adult students tend to be even more proud of the quality and reputation of alma mater—in large part because they feel responsible for their own success, as opposed to traditional students who often are just taking the most logical step forward (and are supported by their parents to do so). And as a recent Eduventures survey shows, nearly one-half of online students prefer to enroll in institutions in their state—where the brand is strongest—and "improved marketing could exploit a market demand for localized online education."[23]

Bottom line: Brand matters—to leadership, to faculty and staff, to students of all types, to alumni, to legislators. And what matters most is that brand intersects with strategic intent.

---

1. 2007 Lipman Hearne/CASE Integrated Marketing Survey.

2. Paul Schervish with John H. Havens, "Why the $41 Trillion Wealth Transfer Estimate Is Still Valid: A Review of Challenges and Questions," *Journal of Gift Planning* 7 (January 2003): 11–15, 47–50.

3. Study by Charles S. Schwab, Aug. 22, 2003, *www.afpnct.org*.

4. Mitch McConnell, on *Face the Nation*, CBS, Feb. 1, 2009.

5. McAlexander, Koenig, and Schouten, "Building Relationships of Brand Community in Higher Education: A Strategic Framework for University Advancement," *International Journal of Educational Advancement* 6 (February 2006): 107–18.

6. Ibid., 108, 111, 112, 115.

7. Lipman Hearne *Key Insights*, April 2007.

8. Lipman Hearne/CASE marketing survey.

9. U.S. Department of Education, Institute of Education Services, National Center for Education Statistics, *Projections of Education Statistics to 2014* (Washington, DC, September 2005).

10. U.S. Department of Education, Institute of Education Services, National Center for Education Statistics, *Projections of Education Statistics to 2017* (Washington, DC, September 2008), table 26, "Actual and projected percentage changes in public high school graduates, by region and state: Selected years, 1999–2000 through 2017–18," *nces.ed.gov/programs/projections/projections2017/tables/table_26.asp?referrer=list*.

11. Henry Tamara, "Report: Greater Percentage of Americans Educated," *USA Today*, June 5, 2002.

12. Lipman Hearne, High Achieving Students Survey, April 2007.

13. WICHE, *Knocking at the College Door*, March 2008.

14. *Chronicle of Higher Education*, Sept. 26, 2008.

15. WICHE, *Knocking at the College Door*.

16. *Chronicle of Higher Education*, Nov. 28, 2003.

17. U.S. Census Bureau, 2008, *www.census.gov/population/www/socdemo/age/age_sex_2008.html*.

18. Moody's Global Credit Research, *2009 U.S. Higher Education Outlook*, Jan. 5, 2009.

19. Ibid.

20. Moody's Investors Service, *2007 Higher Education Outlook: Stable Rating Outlook for Sector in 2007; Longer Term Challenges Building*, Industry Outlook report, January 2007, 8–11.

21. Aslanian Group, *Trends in Adult Learning: A 2006 Snapshot, www.aslaniangroup.com/pdfs/trends-in-learning.pdf.*

22. I. Elaine Allen and Jeff Seaman, *Making the Grade: Online Education in the United States, 2006* (Needham, MA: Sloan Consortium, 2006), 9, *www.sloan-c.org/publications/survey/pdf/making_the_grade.pdf.*

23. Andy Guess, "Geography Emerges in Distance Ed," *Inside Higher Ed*, Nov. 28, 2007, *www.insidehighered.com/news/2007/11/28/online#.*

CHAPTER 2

INSTITUTIONAL INTENT

MOST COLLEGES AND UNIVERSITIES have mission statements that go back to their founding. They are generally full of lofty ideals and abstract rhetoric.

Can you link the institution with the snippet of its mission statement?

1. The advancement and education of youth in all manner of good literature, arts, and sciences.

2. To serve society as a center of higher learning.

3. [Educate] men and women of exceptional potential from all backgrounds so that they may seek, value, and advance knowledge, engage the world around them, and lead principled lives of consequence.

4. To provide a balanced, comprehensive education in liberal arts and sciences, fulfilling the highest standards of intellectual excellence.

5. To teach, to serve and to inquire into the nature of things.

6. The preservation, advancement, and dissemination of knowledge.

7. To prepare students to live lives of purpose, thoughtful inquiry, and responsible leadership.

8. To inspire and educate the scholar and leader in each student.

9. To serve society by educating the leaders of tomorrow and extending the frontiers of knowledge.

A. University of California

B. Amherst College

C. Harvard University

D. Reed College

E. University of Richmond

F. Cornell University

G. University of Georgia

H. Albright College

I. University of Washington[1]

The point here is that the essential role of all educational institutions—at least those that operate as nonprofits—is distributed in the tripartite mission of research, education, and service. Different types of institutions weight these three elements according to the fundamental structure and purpose of the institution. Liberal arts institutions favor teaching over research; public institutions place more emphasis on service; Ph.D.-granting institutions stress the importance of scholarship, inquiry, and research; and comprehensive master's institutions try to emphasize all three simultaneously. Which ain't easy.

STRATEGIC PLANNING

More farsighted institutions focus on strategic planning, but all too often that planning simply reiterates mission, embellished with a sprinkling of platitudes couched in language that is broadly acceptable to all. "One state system wants to 'foster collaboration between units.' A major private university wants to be 'the leader in the integration of teaching and research.' A comprehensive university stakes its future on 'increasing access to knowledge resources.'"[2] While these are worthy goals, they are almost as interchangeable as the mission statements cited above, and they don't go very far in helping an institution determine just what, exactly, it can and should offer to the stakeholders it serves.

Another issue that arises when a college or university is in a strategic planning process is that faculty—academics who, by virtue of their tenured positions, are nearly immune to market forces—are not used to thinking about the positioning of their institution within a competitive environment with the same rigor that they bring to their disciplinary studies. To quote a university president with whom we've worked: "Faculty are those who think otherwise." And it's no wonder. Doctoral training is an extended exercise in shattering hypotheses—both yours and those of others in your discipline. If a graduate student or a colleague runs an idea up the flagpole—no matter how carefully wrought it might be—a faculty member defines the job at hand as shooting holes in the fabric. And if that can be done quickly, wittily, and completely, the faculty artilleryman can stroll away whistling and blowing smoke away from the barrel of the rhetorical cannon just employed to blow the idea to smithereens. Theirs is not the job of reassembly; theirs is the job of devastating critique.

If you know this about faculty, you can go into those meetings prepared to be turned into Swiss cheese—but you can also be prepared with the one tool that faculty respect and honor: data. Because faculty can—and as brand ambassadors must—be brought on board in the strategic and marketing planning process. Without their understanding and participation, any such initiative is dead in the water.

Good strategic planning is an artful combination of top-down direction and bottom-up participation. Without the former, the planning process can drift without focus or direction, lacking a star by which to navigate; without the latter, images of captains Queeg or Ahab (leaders who lost their crews while in the grip of a singular, solitary obsession) come to mind. A strategic planning process, properly managed, can also play an important role by making participants more knowledgeable about their market and institutional environment and by aligning them with a commonly held set of goals. At Pomona College, President David Oxtoby assembled seven faculty-led committees that were encouraged to do "blue sky" thinking in strategic areas, without being concerned about the costs of implementation. Their work was then reviewed and processed by a 20-member committee comprising trustees, faculty members, students, and administrators. The resultant plan focused on areas that have impacts collegewide—on the curriculum, international and regional connections, faculty responsibilities, and the student experience—and each area includes very specific recommendations, such as increasing enrollment by up to 150 students and creating a more robust sabbatical system to encourage faculty research. "We felt the process was as important as the final product," said Oxtoby.[3]

Brand Building Begins at Home

A real brand is not something created and packaged. Slick marketing and a catchy tagline shouldn't define who you are. A real brand is unearthed through self-examination and refined through research, then delivered authentically for the market to experience.

Successful branding efforts must reflect who you really are as an institution. Otherwise, you increase the chance of attracting students who are not the right fit for your school. And faculty and staff won't buy in to the branding efforts—and certainly won't reflect them. In short, you will not have a community that lives the brand.

So what are the keys to authenticity in branding? Start by linking your brand promise to your mission statement. What is your institutional purpose? What are its values? Then, use objective market research to help identify your distinctive qualities and evaluate how they will resonate with your audiences. This will help you develop a brand promise that is both true and compelling.

Enlist Your Brand Ambassadors

The brand is the people who comprise your campus community. As you develop any kind of marketing effort, don't forget about marketing to and enlisting the support of internal audiences. It's important to communicate with faculty and staff about the university's strategic plans and marketing initiatives. Help them understand that every action and every piece of communication makes a difference in how the university is perceived.

At St. Edward's University, we use EDDIE Awards (Every Day Demonstrations of Ingenuity and Excellence) to recognize cross-functional teams that complete innovative projects that enhance the student experience and build the brand. Each year, winners get an EDDIE trophy and VIP parking tag (a premium on any campus!). There are many other ways to engage your internal audiences:

• Host launch parties or sneak previews of marketing campaigns so employees can see the marketing before the general public sees it.

• Conduct a "road show" to take your marketing campaign to staff meetings and faculty gatherings.

• Use on-campus marketing elements to extend your campaign to internal audiences and you'll reap the bonus of word-of-mouth buzz. Think about themed T-shirts for students, faculty, and staff; sidewalk art that showcases your new logo or tagline; banners and flyers linked to your advertising; and branded mouse pads or screen savers for staffers.

• Showcase the good news. In the early days of our strategic plan and branding effort, we passed out buttons for everyone on campus to wear when we broke into the top tier of *U.S. News & World Report* rankings. And don't forget to use your internal marketing toolkit of campus e-mails, newsletters, and Web sites.

- Recognize that campus events are an important way to celebrate who you are and to foster community culture. Plan events with specific goals and key messages.
- Uniforms and name tags can be a source of institutional pride. Our physical plant team embarked on its own "branding" campaign by adopting quality apparel embroidered with the university logo to project professionalism and make the team members identifiable to students and visitors.

Never forget that internal audiences are critical to the success of a marketing plan. Fostering internal buy-in to your branding efforts takes work and time, but it can help you recruit loyal ambassadors who live the brand.

Paige Booth
Vice President for Marketing and Enrollment Management
St. Edward's University

The key to strategic planning is that it drives choices by setting priorities and generates healthy discussion around the general and specific impact of those priorities. Strategic planning is a management tool "through which an organization agrees on—and builds commitment among key stakeholders to—priorities which are essential to its mission and responsive to the operating environment."[4]

"At our university, the worst thing you can do is not participate in the strategic plan," asserts Eugene P. Trani, president of Virginia Commonwealth University. "Then you're not going to get any resources."[5]

A typical strategic planning process involves a series of steps:

1. Definition of vision and mission
2. Environmental scan
   a. Internal organizational factors
   b. External environment: economic, social, demographic, political, legal, technological factors
3. Gap analysis: the difference between the current situation and the desired future
4. Benchmarking: establishing reference points for best practices
5. Definition of strategic issues
6. Program definition: goals, action plans, tactics, resource commitment
7. Emergent strategies ("strategic agility")
8. Evaluation of strategy and assessment of performance[6]

Texas Christian University's Larry Lauer emphasizes that the "marketplace trend analysis must be done first to plan everything else the university will do." Moreover, he asserts that "a well-formulated marketing plan actually constitutes strategic planning. ... A comprehensive *strategic* marketing plan should contain all the elements necessary to guide an institution into the future."[7] Lauer specifies the elements that a successful plan must contain:

1. SWOT analysis
2. Mission, values, and vision
3. Environmental scan
4. Academic program plan
5. Services plan
6. Physical master plan
7. Financial plan
8. Institutional goals
9. Communication plan[8]

FINANCIAL REALITIES

Perhaps the key factor that drives strategy for colleges and universities today is the downstream sustainability of the revenue model. Moody's focus on longer term issues in higher education—mostly around "increasing challenges ... related to shifts in student demand in some areas, reduced affordability, asset/liability management, federal and state support and oversight, and governance reform"[9]—should raise concerns.

And it's not just the bond rating agencies that are worried about the financial squeeze. With the discount rate for private institutions hovering near 40 percent,[10] the average appropriation per full-time student in the nation's public institutions dropping by nearly 8 percent from 2002 to 2007,[11] student tuition accounting for a larger and larger portion of the institution's revenues, Congress looking askance at institutional endowment spending policies, and families growing ever more concerned about the cost/value equation in their matriculation decision, we're on the fringe of a financial "perfect storm" in the funding of institutions of higher learning.

But in that storm, a strong brand can be a great lifeboat—or better yet, a lighthouse perch from which to watch the maelstrom while sipping a cup of tea.

GETTING STARTED: IDENTITY AND BRAND COMMUNICATIONS AUDIT

Too often, *brand* gets confused with *identity*, and the brand discussion gets bogged down in an extended conversation about the logo, type treatment, stationery, and (lately) Web home page. And when the brand conversation is not about the identity, it's often just about how the brand is expressed through communication channels—from presidential speeches to the alumni magazine, from recruitment materials to annual reports, from Web 2.0 to press releases.

Here's the confusing part: Brand is about much more than identity and communications, but an audit of those aspects is a necessary place to start. Think of it this way: If brand is the whole person—living, breathing, working, eating—then identity is the thumbprint and communications is the clothing. That thumbprint, properly managed, will be a consistent identifier for the institution in every context in which it is manifested and the clothing will change based upon the context, activity, and company, but the essence of the person will remain unchanged.

Some Words About Brand Icons

Brand icons are those visible artifacts—signature buildings, recognizable public art, athletic uniforms, but, mostly, logos—that are commonly and irrevocably associated with your brand. I often think of the institutional logo or identity mark as holding the same relationship to the institution that my thumbprint holds to me: It is clearly mine and mine alone, and it's able to distinguish me from others of the species, but it does not in itself contain the whole "me-ness" of *me*. It is, perhaps, not an accident that the nonprofit brand that annually receives "most trusted" status in national surveys has its logo usage rules described in and mandated by the Geneva Convention:

American Red Cross

In the higher education sphere, a number of logos are nationally recognized; some logos are only established in a narrower market context. Each logo, though, triggers a coherent set of responses and associations among its stakeholders.

But icons don't stop with the logo. In the consumer world, millions of dollars are pumped into establishing a series of related visual or sensory icons that all trigger awareness of the parent brand. McDonald's, for example, counts among its icons

the famous golden arches, Ronald McDonald, the Hamburgler (never as popular as Ronald), architectural elements framed around red and gold, the ubiquitous Happy Meals box, and the tunes associated with the advertising taglines "I'm lovin' it" and "You deserve a break today." (I'm betting you can hum either of them, without stopping to think. And why shouldn't you? McDonald's invests hundreds of millions of dollars annually to create awareness around these brand icons.)

Nike, also one of the world's powerful consumer brands, paid only $35 for the Swoosh, but it spends billions annually in associating that mark with charismatic world-class athletes (Michael Jordan, Roger Federer, Maria Sharapova) who reinforce the natal link to Nike, the Greek goddess of victory. So when Michael, Roger, or Maria are in the public eye, they are iconic; they are Nike.

So questions arise. Is our logo coherent? Does it exist in a consistent and appropriate system of usage? What—in addition to our logo—are our icons? Is one of them Old Main? The statue of Long John Frontiersman in the middle of the quad? The Old Well with its store of myths and legends? The library steps? Touchdown Jesus? The athletics or spirit logo? The bust of the founder with its rubbed-smooth-for-luck brass nose? The banana slug in reading glasses? Cataloguing them is critical; assessing when and how to use them is necessary; protecting their value is a continuing responsibility.

And if your institution boasts a score or a hundred competing identities—it's time to take charge.

An identity and brand communications audit starts with collecting published materials from throughout the institution, including both print and digital execution. At a smaller, liberal arts college with a centralized communication function, these materials are often in reasonable accord with each other (though renegade off-brand materials can always be found), but the situation is typically very different at larger master's or research/doctoral institutions. In fact, there's a formulation for this confusion, drawn from my cousin Gordon Moore's dictum that computing power will double in capacity every two years while being halved in cost. My version? Off-brand communications quadruple in direct proportion to the size of the institution. A university with 20,000 students, nine schools, and 16 centers of excellence will have four times the dreck out in the market as an institution half its size. Or maybe quintuple. Often, the lines between institutional identity and athletic identity have been obliterated. These factors—along with the generation of myriad competing logos—make many institutions' identity programs a completely undisciplined mess. And a chaotic identity system will bring confusion to the market from the get-go.

So how have we gotten to this level of identity confusion? Historically, institutions of higher education have become great by giving deans and directors a significant measure of autonomy. "Hire the best people, innovate, maintain quality, and generate revenue" are typically the operating instructions for academic leadership. It's the unusual academic leader who doesn't want his or her own unique identity—frequently one that neglects to mention the parent institution. Identity adherence hasn't been a "qualification" for the deanery, but as more and more institutions begin to recognize the importance of and police the use of a coherent identity system, success in the market will begin to drive the desired behavior. Strengthening the overall brand will help bring these mavericks back into the corral, but the starting point is always assessment of what is.

Identity Audit

An identity audit begins with a comprehensive scan of the identity marks that are currently in circulation, including the institutional seal, the marketing or consumer identity, logos or marks of schools or institutes, the alumni association and/or foundation identity, the athletic identity, and any other variations that exist. Applications on letterhead and business cards, printed materials, Web execution, signage, nomenclature and associated type treatments, and licensed goods are collected. If an identity standards manual exists, that also needs to be assessed both for its coverage of the various needs and options of the institution and for how well it's being followed. Often, it's helpful to gather a similar set of materials from competing or aspirant institutions, and then to put together a document that compares your institutional examples with that of your peers. Although this is not quantitative data, the exercise accomplishes much the same purpose with faculty and administrative leaders by providing both the institutional and the competitive context.

The criteria by which an identity program is assessed include:

- Consistency: Is the identity applied in a consistent manner across all applications? Can the identity be deployed in a variety of ways (horizontal, stacked, etc.)?
- Usage: Are the right marks deployed in the appropriate situations (i.e., is the official seal with a religious motif imprinted on the bottom of an ashtray)? Is there clarity of application—with the seal used for formal settings, the consumer mark used in marketing activities, and the athletic mark(s) used in sports-related materials?
- Brand relevance: Does the identity signal key brand attributes?
- Hierarchy: Does the identity allow colleges, schools, departments, and other units to establish their own identities—and at the same time signal their place in the organizational structure?
- Application/production issues: Does the identity work in color? In black and white? Is it scalable? Does it work as a fax cover sheet? Is it effective in signage? Does it work in a digital environment?
- Content: If there is a tagline(s), is usage consistent? Does the tag connect with the visual identity? With the institutional brand?

Brand Communications Audit

The process of beginning a brand communications audit must start with a definition of what *brand communications* actually are. For the purposes of developing an understanding of how your brand is being communicated—without getting too deep in the weeds of looking at all communications from every department, directorate, and homegrown designer on campus—brand communications are those that 1) attempt to speak for the whole institution, 2) are targeted at broad-based segments of the institution's stakeholders, such as prospective students, alumni, donors, community leaders and other influencers, etc., 3) are tied to the president's or chancellor's vision, the strategic plan, or other institutional positioning directives, and 4) are or become the touchstones from which other, more isolated, communications are derived.

From this perspective, brand communications would include the viewbook and related student recruitment collateral; the annual or president's report; the strategic plan (if published); the president's "state of the institution" speeches and other major addresses; capital campaign materials, if the institution is in a public campaign setting; the alumni or "friends" magazine; primary and secondary Web pages, including the landing page, and pages built to accommodate the needs and interests of prospective and current students, faculty and staff, alumni, donors, and media representatives; and image advertising. This material needs to be reviewed with three criteria in mind: consistency, alignment, and benefit.

Consistency

While each particular communication tool will be shaped by its purpose and its audience (obviously, a search piece aimed at a 16-year-old National Merit finalist will be different in tone and imagery than a planned giving brochure sent to that student's grandmother), they should all spring from a shared understanding of the particular character, promise, and role of the institution. If, for example, the recruitment materials focus on the intimacy of the environment and the relationship between faculty and students, and the annual report stresses only the institutional profile as a powerhouse of cutting-edge research, the disconnect is obvious. Anybody looking at the whole institution would have to ask: Does this organization really know what it's doing, why it exists? Can it possibly deliver on these divergent promises? Can we trust these folks to do what they say?

Another important aspect of consistency is *duration*: How long has your institution been pounding on its core brand message, and what evidence do you have that the message is getting through? David Ogilvy, one of the 20th century's true innovators in communications, is widely attributed to have said that there are three important things about advertising: "Repetition. Repetition. Repetition." And the same can be said for brand communications. (Did I mention? The same can be said for brand communications.)

Messages are not just verbal. Your stakeholders form as much of an impression from the visual as from the rhetorical—if not more. Is the photography or other imagery consistent with the language? Does it send an appropriate message—of quality, or of spontaneity, or of artful construction? Does the imagery support or undercut the intent of the heds, subheds, cutlines, captions, and running text? Are the production values consistent with the desired message and appropriate for the venue?

Alignment

The next question is one of alignment. Are the messages in the brand communications—both rhetorical and visual—aligned with the key brand attributes that the institution wants to project? Do you know what those attributes are? (For a more in-depth discussion about analyzing and employing those attributes to your benefit, see chapter 5, "Brand Platform.") Or if you don't know what those attributes are—if you haven't used *The Real U* to your advantage (tsk-tsk)—or your institution hasn't gone through a real process of understanding your brand in its marketplace context, ask yourself and your colleagues: What would somebody who doesn't know anything about us assume to be true about us if they only had these materials as a guide?

A useful exercise in this regard is to assemble the materials that meet the criteria for brand communications (institutionwide, broad audiences, etc.) and search for keywords or phrases that are repeated from channel to channel as if a mantra. Do they exist? Are they consistent across platforms? Do they *align* with the intent of your institution, as you understand them? Do they present an accurate picture of what your institution values? Do they present an accurate picture of what your institution can deliver?

To help with internal buy-in, it's also useful to identify a direct or aspirational competitor or two that is doing a good job with its brand communications. Mount that institution's materials—and yours—on oversized poster board and step back and look at the results. If the other institution's materials present a coherent and focused portrait of the institution, and yours look like the dog's breakfast (a technical term derived from the mixed-together slop of leftovers and dry kibble that's dumped in the pooch's bowl), then you've gone a long way toward identifying the problem and beginning to rally support for the desired solution.

Benefit

This may be the hardest criterion to assess, because it requires you to get outside of yourself and see your institution as others see it. All too often, internal complacency sets in and drives the messaging: This is who we are, this is what we value, this is why we're so darn wonderful—now why aren't you responding?

In fact, *benefit* is a term that applies only to the audience, not to the speaker. It doesn't matter why you think you provide value to the world (or certain key stakeholder elements of it); it only matters what benefit those stakeholders derive from you, in terms that they set and measure. And this is not something that insiders can easily see, particularly those who have been steeped for years in their own projected institution-speak. For much of the last half of the 20th century, the higher education sector has been remarkably oblivious to market forces. The exception occurred in the 1950s and 1960s, when many "pure" liberal arts colleges (of which there was an oversupply) added business, allied health, and other pre- and professional programs in order to survive and thrive. On the whole, however, higher education has been able to continue to increase supply in accord with demand for the past 50 years. And the professoriate, the inmates who in many ways run the asylum (or should I say the intellects who illuminate the "shining city on the hill"), has been even more insulated than have been the administrators by virtue of this thing called tenure.

So, how do outsiders determine institutional benefit? Or, more to the point, how do you learn what value they see in your institution? There's a simple answer: You ask. (See chapter 3, "A Sense of Where You Are," for a detailed discussion of market research.) The quickest and most reliable method is to use focus groups, which offer moderated, institution-blind discussions with key stakeholder groups of you and your competitors, starting with awareness and building through perception, then diving into "takeaways" based on communications materials that the moderator distributes to inform the discussion. Being behind the glass in a well-directed focus group, observing how people actually relate to and feel about your brand, can be hugely instructive, as will be seen in the following pages.

Just remember: You're researching this to inform your brand strategy; it's not just finding out for the sake of finding out. And the ultimate goal is to find a way to effectively position your institution in the marketplace so you can reach mission-critical institutional goals. Which leads to my first aphorism: "Strategic planning without market differentiation is just wishful thinking."

1. 1-C, 2-A, 3-B, 4-D, 5-G, 6-I, 7-E, 8-H, 9-F

2. Roger L. Williams, "Out with the Old, In with the New," CURRENTS 26 (January 2000): 64.

3. Paul Fain, "'Blue Sky' Planning Opens the Floor to Ideas at Pomona," *Chronicle of Higher Education*, Oct. 5, 2007.

4. Michael Allison and Jude Kaye, *Strategic Planning for Nonprofit Organizations: A Practical Guide and Workbook* (New York: Wiley, 1997), 1.

5. Paul Fain, "Vision for Excellence," *Chronicle of Higher Education*, Oct. 5, 2007.

6. Alexandra L. Learner, "A Strategic Planning Primer for Higher Education," paper prepared for the College of Business Administration and Economics, California State University, July 1999, 7-9, *www.atlm.edu/irpa/publications/Strategic_Planning_Primer.pdf*.

7. Larry Lauer, *Advancing Education in Uncertain Times* (Washington, DC: CASE, 2006), 45.

8. Ibid., 51–52.

9. Moody's Investors Service, *2007 Higher Education Outlook: Stable Rating Outlook for Sector in 2007; Longer Term Challenges Building*, Industry Outlook report, January 2007, 1.

10. NACUBO, Tuition Discounting Survey, May 2009.

11. Scott Jaschik, "Good Years Before the Bad," *Inside Higher Ed*, Feb. 28, 2008, *www.insidehighered/news/2008/02/28/approps#*.

CHAPTER 3

A SENSE OF
WHERE YOU ARE

IN THE HEADY HEYDAY OF ADVERTISING, when every new jingle bored into American gray matter like a hookworm and rampant consumerism was just discovering its own awesomeness, Rosser Reeves further crystallized the fundamental notion that David Ogilvy had been developing since he first worked on the Aga Cooker account: that of the Unique Selling Proposition, or USP. The theory of the USP is simple: Find that singular element of your product or service that no one else can duplicate, that is yours alone, around which you can build your entire marketing premise—then hammer that home, relentlessly.

In the education sector, we run into issues around the first word of that formulation: *unique*. After all, how many "offers" in education are truly unique, unduplicated in terms that are valued by the market? The answer: very few.

Of course, you can always find the "unique" in the USP by reducing it to its core, locational features: "Credenza University is the finest university on the intersection of Main and College Streets in Credenza, Ohio." But once the attributes of location are removed—and those are only decision drivers for a limited few—most colleges and universities fall back into reciting key characteristics of their *category*. Consider the following statements of three fierce competitors in the "liberal arts plus category" (all trumpeted as the "why consider us" rationale on their Web sites). Names have been obscured to protect the undifferentiated.

> The University of XXYYZZ is a leading
> liberal arts institution for students who seek
> both the intimacy of a small college and the
> academic, research, and cultural opportunities
> of a large university.

XXYYZZ University is one of the top
liberal arts colleges in the nation, but
beyond our broad liberal arts college curriculum
we also offer strong professional programs.
We are one of the few institutions in the nation
that successfully combines the personal attention
of a small college with the
academic resources of a large university.

XXYYZZ University combines the personalized attention
of a small, liberal arts college with the
resources, technology, and co-curricular
opportunities of a large university.

Other than it took the middle institution twice the verbiage to state the same essential proposition (and we edited), what—according to these statements—really differentiates these three fine, successful institutions from one another? The answer, with the brand power of the names themselves taken out: "I dunno." These statements successfully put forward the features of the category, but not of the specific institution itself. They are infused with a somewhat self-congratulatory sense of "telling you what we want you to know" rather than expressing the more primal, emotional values of the brand. They clearly present certain category features, but are indistinguishable in terms of the *lived experience*—the actual character of the individual institution. And while establishing the benefits of the category is important, it ranks relatively low on the brand-value scale. You have to do more than trumpet the merits of the group to which you belong—narrowing the field but not drawing the prospect to you.

All research/doctoral institutions conduct cutting-edge research in one arena or another—or claim to. All of them offer interaction—limited or extensive—between researchers and students and provide opportunities for students to be involved in research or scholarly initiatives. But if you're in this set, you must answer this specific question: Why do *you* matter?

All comprehensive universities try to position themselves as the "just right" option between impersonal mega-universities and limiting small colleges, with enough range of subject matter and variety of opportunity to suit those students who desire a larger playing field. Generally, these institutions also focus on a handful of specialties—either arrived at serendipitously by the efforts of key faculty members or strategically by focusing on local or regional needs—and tout their leadership in those areas. But what is the specific importance of what you do to the markets in which you're engaged?

All liberal arts colleges talk about small classrooms, close contact with professors, and a singular dedication to the undergraduate experience. Properly enunciated, these are strong category attributes. But how does your institution act them out? What's different about your approach or outcomes from the approach or outcomes of your top competitors? What is embedded in your institutional DNA?

To get more specific, you have to go deeper into your own distinctive reality, honestly assessing what you have or do that makes you different, that makes you, in your competitive context, unique. And from this you will develop (watch out! here comes another marketing term) your *positioning*. There's a basic definition of the term *positioning* from which all the art and science of brand strategy spring: "how you differentiate your product in the mind of your prospect."[1] Obviously, in academe, *product* is a suspect term; but exchange *service* or *institution* or *experience* for *product* and the point is clear. What matters is how your stakeholders—be they alumni, influencers, other educators, legislators, faculty, staff, students, prospective students, or parents of prospective students—perceive you, how they value what you offer.

Consider the case of the mid-tier private "liberal arts plus" institution that finds itself competing primarily with significantly larger public entities. In this case, the language of "intimacy" and "personal attention" will be far more compelling than if that institution were competing with other institutions that offered essentially the same features. But even in this instance, the pitch would have to do more than simply sell the category. Characteristics of the institutional personality—the peculiar and distinctive thumbprint of the institution itself—would have to be explored and integrated into the brand presentation (for details, see chapter 5, "Brand Platform"). But this process all starts with positioning—the role or value or space in which *prospect* has placed you, which may or may not be consistent with the role or value you think you deserve or offer.

And always remember, differentiation is the key to positioning. If your prospect can't tell the difference between your institution and its competitors, you're asking the prospect to make a decision or take an action without the ability to discern between your offer and others that are potentially equally valid. "Differentiation is one of the most important strategic and tactical activities in which [institutions] constantly engage," writes Harvard management guru Theodore Levitt. "It is not discretionary."[2]

So the questions you have to answer:

- Who are your real (primary) competitors? In what context? In what markets?
- What truly distinguishes your institution from those competitors?
- How is this distinction valued in the minds of your prospects?
- What will it take for you to validate that distinction externally?
- What will it take for you to convince internal audiences about the need for emphasizing and delivering on that distinction?

In classic marketing terms, positioning is derived from the interplay of three forces: institutional capacity and intent, competitive context, and marketplace perception. Let's take these forces one at a time.

INSTITUTIONAL CAPACITY AND INTENT

An earlier chapter laid out some basics of assessing and deriving institutional intent through a strategic planning process (a subject worthy of a book unto itself). All too often, though, strategic planning is set aside in favor of another, more popular, discipline: wishful thinking. That's where an assessment of institutional capacity comes in—conducted with ruthless, clear-eyed objectivity. Myriad reference sources can categorize for you the research and resource prowess of all your departments. Your institutional research guru can tell you, in exhaustive detail, demographics and trendlines of your student body in terms of admission, retention, household income, and postgraduate professional affiliation. Your VP for business and finance can tell you (in all likelihood with comparable data for competing or aspirant institutions) about funding sources and allocations. Economic forecasting and employment statistics can give you a sense of job demand in the coming decade. NSSE can tell you what your first-year students expect from you and what your fourth-year students believe they got. Alumni can tell you—through their participation in events, their support for your initiatives, and the pattern of their contributions—what they think about their time with you and what they think about what you've done since they left. Comparative staffing exercises with other institutions can tell you how well-prepared you are, in relative terms, to engage in a comprehensive brand initiative. Pull it all together. Then pour yourself another cup of coffee. You're only beginning.

COMPETITIVE CONTEXT

In the great majority of cases, competitive context is focused primarily on the enrollment market. For highly selective institutions, with strongly defined brands and prodigious resources, the competitive context might be more concerned with faculty recruitment, sponsored research prowess, global reputation, or other criteria not centered in the student market. Almost universally, though, revenues from students—whether from tuition and fees, per capita distributions from state coffers, sponsored public or private scholarship support, or room and board payments—make up the lion's share of institutional revenue. So we'll concentrate our discussion of competitive context on enrollment issues for the same reason that Willie Sutton said he robbed banks: because that's where the money is.

Determining your key enrollment competitors is fairly simple. Your admissions office should maintain a registry of cross-apps: the other schools to which your prospects applied. They will also have a "bump" list that tallies the win/loss ratio against each of these competitors. If you win the majority of the time, don't worry for now about these institutions. If you lose the majority of the time, these institutions are the initial targets for your competitive analysis. These will probably *not* be the competitors that your administration would prefer; almost invariably, if asked to name competitors, your president or provost will name a number of schools significantly higher in the academic pecking order. It's an ego thing related to Groucho's observation that "I wouldn't want to be a member of any club that would admit me." But that's OK; your branding initiative is going to serve the purpose of elevating your enrollment profile and bringing you into competition with a new set of worthy institutions—and you'll have to position yourself to compete with them. Typically, you should investigate a set of six competitor institutions: two or three from the top current cross-app list and the remainder from either aspirant institutions (those that most resemble "who we'd like to be") or institutions a bit deeper in your cross-app list, where you lose even more consistently.

First, develop a grid for you and your competitors, listing the observable, measurable comparisons such as those that could be found in *U.S. News & World Report* or other outside agencies: test scores of entering students, retention and graduation rates, student FTE, tuition/fees, percent receiving financial aid and level of aid, faculty/student ratio, etc. Next, amplify the comparison by looking at purely "product" issues: number of majors, strength of departments, graduate placement rates by discipline, and the like. Finally, and most fun, launch a secret shopper comparison by calling or e-mailing the admissions office of each competitor—as well as your own—and presenting them a profile of a desirable student: excellent SAT scores, salutatorian, striker on the soccer team, flugelhorn player. Make all the calls on the same day, and be prepared to record both the objective and subjective information you derive. Was your call answered by a person? Did the person seem to care about you? Was appropriate information forthcoming? Did you feel the beginning of a relationship? Did a sense of the brand, as lived, start to come through?

As the materials start to arrive, maintain your tally. On what day did the materials land in your mailbox? Were they addressed to you or to "applicant"? First-class or third-class postage? Signed or form letter? Were the enclosures responsive to your applicant's profile?

Now, dig into the materials themselves. What is your overall impression? What does the imagery suggest? Are the materials energetic, personal, accessible? Flip through the pages (this is what your prospects will do). What do the headlines and captions tell you about the institution? What would you conclude—after 30 arduous seconds of investigation (what your prospects will give you on first pass-through)—about this institution? What key messages stand out—repeated mantras, prominent statements supported by quotes from smiling students or faculty, charts or graphs that attempt to validate claims? Objectively, what are these institutions saying about themselves? Subjectively, what's the tone or personality that the institution is trying to project? Think back to the idea of brand as narrative: What is the story that is being conveyed? And, most important, would you feel compelled to read further, or would you toss the materials into the 70-pound pile that's already accumulated next to your desk? If not, the materials don't meet their purpose.

Finally, write a brief positioning statement for each institution, based on what you can garner from all the touch points you've had: the way the phone was answered, the materials themselves, any follow-up efforts that the institution made in the subsequent days and weeks. Frame it as "More than any other institution, (*institution name here*) is better able to (*distinct, verifiable opportunity/impact here*) for (*target audience here*)." Make sure to include your own institution in that comparison set. Then ask yourself: Are we sufficiently distinct from our competition? Are we all in a muddle together? Is there some kind of a conceptual gap—

an opportunity to highlight aspects of what we offer—that the competitive set does not fill? Does this gap potentially provide us a real market advantage?

But before you get too locked into this potential advantage, you have to consider the third element of positioning: how you are perceived in the marketplace. And this requires research.

MARKETPLACE PERCEPTION

Donna Van De Water, who leads the Lipman Hearne research team, has taught me that there's only one question to ask when you are thinking of launching a research initiative: What do you want to *do* with the data? *Not*: What do you want to know? We're all curious beasts, easily distracted by learning new, peculiar "truths." *Not*: I've always wondered … We all wonder, and will always, and research is too time-consuming and expensive to be designed to satisfy someone's idle curiosity—unless, of course, that someone is the president of your institution or a deep-pockets trustee. In which case, call me. (Kidding!)

But if you ask yourself, What do I want to *do* with the data? you can present a problem with a purpose to your research team. Knowing the action that is under consideration, knowing how the data will inform that action, is the single most important key to getting good research results.

Asking the Right Questions

Qual or quant? Survey or focus group? In person or online? What's right for us?

We know that the difference between success and failure lies in good decision-making. Market research provides tools to make informed decisions and keep institutions at the top of their games. Experience, sound judgment, and research combine for effective decision-making.

We take a practical approach to research. We believe research must begin with an end in mind. We need to determine not just the infor- mation that's sought, but how it's to be used and by whom. Managers who are going to make effective use of research need to take a role in deciding among the many research choices and options. There are three broad research models: exploratory, descriptive, and causal. Sometimes you need one; sometimes you need more for a complete picture.

Exploratory research is the least structured and most flexible of the three models. Usually the number of participants is small and only partially representative of your constituency. In the world of branding and marketing, we think of qualitative techniques when the exploratory model is called for, including:

• Secondary data (e.g., literature searches, census data, industry reports, papers and talks from conferences, and previously conducted research)

• Individual interviews with industry experts and knowledge leaders

• Case studies

• Focus groups (and their variants including dyads and triads, online and face-to-face)

• Depth interviews

• Ethnographic studies

• Photo ethnography

These techniques provide a mix of perspectives that are great for generating new creative ideas, uncovering constituent needs and attitudes, and testing new products and services. All are useful for understanding and defining problems and specifying information needs or in planning further, more rigorous research. They can also be used at the back end of a research study, to help amplify quantitative conclusions and make recommendations from survey data.

Descriptive research is appropriate in situations where, because of previous research or a strong hunch, you understand the questions facing the institution and need to decide among possible responses or quantify a particular factor. In general terms, descriptive research attempts to determine the frequency with which something occurs, or to discover the relationship between two or more factors—important because decision-making is complex. This model is a little more scientific and less flexible than exploratory research.

When you need to establish a cause-and-effect relationship, it's time to turn to the third model, experimental research. Descriptive and experimental models usually fall in the quantitative bucket. Qualitative research investigates the depth and range of constituent attitudes and beliefs. It does not measure incidence, nor does it project or forecast quantity. That's the role of quantitative research, which uses sampling strategies (and the occasional census) to project results to the population of interest. Quantitative research helps uncover insights; qualitative helps us understand why it's happening. Frequently used quantitative methods include:

• Online surveys

• Personal interviews

• Mail surveys

• Telephone surveys

Appropriately designed surveys allow you to conduct a range of analyses to uncover insights driving brand, including basic cross-tabulations, multivariate analyses, regression, discriminant analysis, factor analysis, and multidimensional scaling.

The recommendation of one survey approach over another will depend upon the research objective, time requirements, sample availability, nature of the constituent group of interest, and quality control issues. In general, it's safe to use online approaches with constituents close to the institution (e.g., faculty and staff, current students, alumni) and if you are confident you'll have a truly representative sample. For constituents who may be less familiar with the institution or for whom you can't be assured of a representative sample, you may need to consider other approaches. Sometimes it's necessary to use a hybrid approach, combining two or more quantitative methods to optimize response or measurement validity.

Donna Van De Water
Managing Director and Principal
Lipman Hearne

Qualitative Methods

Begin with qualitative research to determine what the underlying perceptions and issues are from the audience's perspective. Without such intake, you run the danger of not asking the right questions in the broader, more expensive, and more durable quantitative research. In qualitative research, segmentation remains important, with screeners—either used by professional focus group facilities or developed by your own admissions or advancement staff (depending on the purpose of the groups)—being employed to make sure the participants represent the point of view that is being explored. These screeners might be built to identify prospective students who fit the desired profile of applicants (sometimes separated into male and female groups);

alumni with donor, lybunt, or nondonor status; significant influencers, such as science teachers, coaches, or admissions counselors; parents of prospective students; or other segments—each with enough consistency that a focus group report could state, with confidence, "high achieving male prospects believe ..." based on the collective responses of those focus groups.

A skilled moderator is paramount, as it's often necessary to balance the dynamic of the group—not allowing one or two headstrong and voluble individuals (technically known in the trade as "blowhards") to dominate or intimidate the group, encouraging involvement and soliciting contributions by all participants. The moderator should be working from a discussion guide that's consistent from group to group so that the varying perspectives of different segments can be balanced and compared.

Other forms of qualitative research—individual interviews, discussion groups, online discussion or focus groups, bulletin boards, and chat—need to follow this same model: careful segmentation, a consistent discussion guide, a reporting format that allows for both summary analysis and verbatim commentary. With that as a basis, qualitative research can go a long way toward answering nuanced, dimensional needs for market perspective.

After the qualitative research has confirmed or refined institutional understanding of the general market impression, it's time to get gritty with the numbers. Calling all quant jockeys!

Behind the Glass

Being behind the glass at a focus group can be one of the most important and meaningful ways for your institutional representatives to intersect with your markets. There's nothing like the experience of seeing who "they" are—how they dress, what they know, what they think is smart or funny or insightful—to underscore how you are perceived. It can be frustrating at times, though. I remember one focus group for a mid-tier private university in the American Midwest, attended by the institution's president. The prospective students in the group—all drawn from the inquirers' pool at the institution—agreed that the university was public: "Yep, it's public." The president had to be restrained from banging on the glass and shouting "You're wrong! You're wrong!" but he learned something about the impression that his communications program had been creating.

Quantitative Methods

Quantitative research serves many purposes, not the least of which is that—more than any other single factor—it has the power to move minds on campus. Earlier in this book, I wrote about faculty skepticism about branding, marketing, and other disciplines that carry with them a whiff of consumerism, product puffery, and shameless promotion (*n.b.*: I don't believe these to be the characteristics of a smart, well-founded marketing program, but this is a prejudice marketers often encounter on campus). "Faculty," as aphorized earlier, "are those who think otherwise." But faculty are smart, and they are accustomed to dealing with data—and nothing is more powerful in terms of "unsticking" their long-held beliefs than a bulletproof data set, compellingly presented.

Historically, the means to gain quantitative market data were limited to mail or telephone-based surveys, or occasionally massive "intercept" surveys at stores, malls, sporting events, concerts, or other venues where the target gathers. Since the birth of the Web, additional means are available, but all have their strengths and weaknesses.

Telephone surveys have the advantage of convenience. Once you've completed all your interviews of a particular segment—such as 100 high-achieving college-bound females in the Northeast—you can stop collecting data from that segment and concentrate your resources on the collection of data from comparable segments. There are issues, though. In an era of cell phones and caller I.D., it's harder to get through to the appropriate respondents. There are also demographic questions: Does the profile of those who would answer a call from a marketing research organization match the profile of the group you're trying to survey? There are also timing questions: The questionnaire can't reasonably ask for the respondent to stay on the telephone for more than 12 to 15 minutes or compare complex sets of variables without diminishing the quality of the response—and, obviously, testing visual creative is impossible over the phone.

Mail surveys enable the researcher to ask more questions that require ranking, relative ratings or scores, or evaluation of a series of nuanced statements that may require review and reflection for the respondent to provide a valid answer. Mail surveys, though, are cumbersome, time-intensive, subject to relatively low response rates (and often require follow-up prompts or other incentives), and in need of extensive data-input and coding after the results are in.

Web-based surveys are both time- and cost-efficient, but they are also potentially subject to demographic skew. Is the audience you're targeting comfortable on the Web? Is your Web-ready sample consistent with the overall sample, or will certain segments (younger alumni, for example) respond more fully? Is the person actually filling out the survey the one you're trying to reach, or is someone else accessing the survey through the Web link?

Whatever quantitative method you use should be driven by Donna's question: What do you want to do with the data? And whatever method you use, you should employ two techniques to further reinforce the validity of the data you generate.

First, before you field the full survey, go out with a small sample beta-test of the instrument and the method. Do any issues regarding the questionnaire surface during the beta test, such as the audience's ability to respond appropriately to the questions, the length of the survey, or other problems that might make your job harder after the full survey is fielded and completed?

And second, after the survey is back from the field, compare its results to other survey work that you've done and to other relevant public survey data. Do your results fit within what we know about the market in general? Do your respondents share similarities (or explainable differences) with the respondents to broad general surveys? How can the comparison of these different data sets improve your analysis?

WHEN TO TEST

In general, research plans can be formulated in one of two ways:

- Exploratory: to establish benchmarks in terms of awareness, perception, understanding, and usage among key audience segments—typically to inform positioning and/or to provide a baseline as an ambitious, multiyear marketing initiative is launched
- Validation: to test/validate hypotheses about institutional positioning and/or to garner responses to creative concepts or other brand expressions

Exploratory research typically requires both qualitative and quantitative methods. Qualitative methods get at nuance, emotional content, and greater texture through one-on-one interviews, discussion groups, and focus groups (in-person and online); quantitative methods derive the kind of statistical certainty about awareness, attitude, and knowledge on a segment-by-segment basis that is the basis for downstream measurement of campaign effectiveness. Exploratory research is typically broad-based and intended to provide fundamental understanding about marketplace perceptions that will be addressed in a comprehensive marketing campaign.

Validation research might just as well be called (in)validation research because its function is to test the validity (or lack thereof) of positioning options, creative concepts, ads or other brand expression materials. Sometimes this round of research is used after a more exhaustive exploratory phase has been completed; in other instances, if a detailed and rigorous analysis of institutional capacity and competitive context has been completed, the brand team can leap forward to hypothetical positioning options that seem to be available to the institution, and assess how well or poorly those options resonate in the marketplace—and how well or poorly they are seen to fit with the institution itself.

In any case, the planning for any research initiative should be driven by Donna's question (repeat after me): What are you going to do with the data? It's too important, and too expensive, and too visible, and too time-consuming to launch a major research program without that clear-eyed focus on the goal.

ONE FINAL WORD ABOUT DIFFERENTIATION

Remember, through your positioning work, you're trying to arrive at one key understanding: how you differentiate your institution in its competitive set. Evolving from that understanding is the brand platform that will inform all your branding and marketing communications efforts. But differentiation has to be based on the values of the marketplace you're trying to affect. Consider these two formulas:

$$Differentiation - Value = Inertia$$

$$Differentiation + Value = Sustainable\ Competitive\ Advantage$$

And value, in institutional branding, is based on another formula:

$$Value = Experience \div Cost$$

People are willing to pay more for an experience that promises—and then delivers—against lofty expectations. Not too surprisingly, cost can become almost a nonfactor when talking about the lives and future prospects of the students who take us up on our offer. So the brand experience—what you actually deliver in the classroom and the residence hall, on the playing field and in the career services office—must be of as high a quality as possible. For over-delivering is a far surer path to success than underpricing. Again, we turn to Professor Levitt: "There is no reason for any [institution] to get stuck in the commodity trap, forever confined to competing totally on price alone. Historically, [institutions] that have taken and stayed resolutely on the commodity path ... have become extinct."[3]

So, if extinction is not the path you want to take, read on ...

---

1. Jack Trout, *Differentiate or Die* (New York: John Wiley & Sons, 2000), 73.

2. Theodore Levitt, *Thinking About Management* (New York: Free Press, 1991), 134.

3. Ibid., 134.

CHAPTER 4

BRAND BASICS

THERE'S A GREAT LINE CREDITED TO BO DIDDLEY that expressly captures the most important aspect of any brand claim: "Don't let your mouth write no checks that your a∗∗ can't cash."[1] True as this might be, that particular "a" word is not the one that is most important in terms of brand. Instead, that word is *authenticity*.

AUTHENTICITY

In a brand, authenticity is the guarantee that the institution is actually able to deliver on the promise that it makes. It's the proof to faculty—those who think otherwise—that the brand initiative is actually founded on the lived reality of the institution, on those elements that they have come to know and value in their work with colleagues and with students and in their community service. It's the proof to students—who had certain expectations when they made their enrollment decision—that they made the right choice. It's the assurance to alumni that the place they know, the place where they made an important step forward on the highway of life, the place whose name is on their c.v. and on their spirit T-shirts, still knows itself and provides real, discernable value today.

Think about it. When Yugo was making a run at the American car market a few years back, it didn't try to base its appeal on the core brand concept of "safety." Not only did Volvo own that space in the consumer's mind, but anybody who test drove a Yugo—heard the tinny clang of ill-fitting sheet metal when the doors banged shut or felt the wind from a passing semi bounce the car all over the road—would have quickly rejected the "safety" claim in favor of "cheap," which is, in fact, how Yugo was marketed and sold. And anybody who bought one is probably still experiencing a degree of regret. (Recall Levitt's assertion in the previous chapter about the commodity track and extinction. Who knew the whole country would go down the drain with the death of the car?)

So what does *authenticity* mean in terms of a college or university? It starts with the pure features that are part of your category: small classes or NCAA Division I football, urban grit or bucolic glade, faculty focus on teaching or faculty expectations of groundbreaking research, integrated campus residential community or commuter haven. These features are essentially unchangeable—or changing them, at least, is not generally considered to be the purview of the marketing department. (In corporate settings, marketing often is a driving force in reconsideration of products or services; it is seen as wisdom to configure your business offerings to the needs of the marketplace. In academe, such an approach would be regarded as heretical.)

Authenticity also extends to the expressed personality of your institution. If your student body is very preppy, very social, very Greek, you would be wise not to present your brand characteristics as "maverick" or "the road less traveled." Conversely, if your campus is a haven for the purple-haired and disturbingly pierced, or the drop-in destination for the blue-collar adult commuter, or the hard-edged training ground for the future titan of industry, your branding has to reflect that reality, that lived experience.

All too often, brand marketing messages from an institution radiate almost entirely from the academic enterprise, the intellectual core. But an exercise I often conduct when doing group branding workshops quickly clarifies the problems with this approach. The exercise consists of a series of questions:

In your undergraduate experience, how many of you learned 100 percent of what you know and value in the classroom?

80 percent?

60 percent?

40 percent?

20 percent?

Nobody has ever raised his or her hand at 100 percent—maybe for fear of being quickly derided as a total geek. A few hands go up at 80 percent, and there's a forest of them at 60 percent and 40 percent. So the question extends: Why do you think, for this generation of students, the answer would be any different? And why do you think that giving short shrift to the entire experience—in the residence halls and dining commons, on the athletic courts and fields, in planned meetings and impromptu bull sessions, in the lonely night of the soul—is any way to appeal to a prospective student?

Now, branding is not always about enrollment. Indeed, for a number of institutions, the purpose of a branding initiative is as much or more about influencer or legislative relations, alumni and donor involvement—but these tend to be institutions that arguably already have a strong reputation, if not a well-defined or clearly delineated brand. But for the great majority of institutions, revenue associated with enrollment (including tuition and fees, room and board, incidental expenses, state per capita allocations, endowment returns designated for scholarships and fellowships, etc.) constitutes the great majority of the budget—from 40 percent to

80 percent of all incoming dollars—so being cavalier about prospective students constitutes a perilous path.

To some extent, academe's impulse to focus primarily on the classroom and academic enterprise is an outcome of two structural factors that have built the institution as we know it: first, the demographics that have driven enrollments for much of the past two decades; and second, the mindset that comes with academic tenure. Both of these factors have historically made it easy for academic institutions to ignore or dismiss market forces, except in extreme situations. But that's changing. Demographic changes (presented in depth in chapter 1) and an increased understanding of the validity of effective marketing are having their impact. Over the 10 years that Lipman Hearne has been surveying marketing investments in higher education, the average investment has more than doubled; but it's another, more qualitative, measure that has had an even greater effect. On many campuses, the mantle of "marketing champion" has been taken up by faculty members who recognize that their interests—more and better students, a stronger position for recruiting colleagues, a stronger base for competing for research dollars, and the like—are best served by a strongly branded, distinct, and appreciated institution.

VALUE

Once you've done the work to determine the authenticity of your brand claim, you next have to make sure you position it in terms of value to the marketplace. And value, in marketing terms, remains dependent on that simple formula:

$$Value = Experience \div Cost$$

What this formula points out is that authenticity is great and necessary, but if it's not firmly established in the perceived value structure of the marketplace, it goes nowhere. And the hinge point here, the term around which the formula rotates, is the experience itself: the experience establishes the value. The better the experience, the more you're willing to pay. The more you pay, the greater your expectations of the experience. This is a lesson that other "life experience" brands understand and that higher education would do well to emulate. Consider, if you will, the following fleet of brands, all owned by the same corporation:

Ritz-Carlton

JW Marriott Hotels

Renaissance Hotels

Fairfield Inn

SpringHill Suites

Residence Inn

TownePlace Suites

Road warriors will quickly recognize the difference between a night at the Ritz-Carlton (love that 24/7 room service) and one at the Fairfield Inn (Dang! The vending machine is out of Quaker rice snacks!). The differences are manifold: from construction standards to room appointments, from service staff training and expectations to availability and quality of cuisine. Obviously, when you're booking your rooms for a New York stay, you understand the difference in the brands—you've internalized the experience/cost formula and determined what, to you, provides the most value. Are you looking for a top-of-the-line experience, and are you willing to pay for it? Or do you want to leave more money in your pocket for Broadway shows, dinner at Sardi's, and late night clubbing? (Heck, it's New York. You probably won't spend much time in the room anyway.) And the price points are in line with the formula, with the Manhattan Ritz-Carlton posted at 500 percent of the Fairfield rate, yet the two hotels are only a short cab ride apart.

Perhaps the clearest example of this kind of suite of brands in higher ed is in the state of California, where the 1960 Master Plan for Higher Education specified the structural differences, enrollment criteria, faculty expectations (and pay grades), and price points for institutions in the public sector. Enacting this plan created a well-differentiated environment, one that is understood by the general public. The 10 member institutions of the University of California system are known to be universities that focus on research, boast top-quality graduate and professional programs, admit only the top 10 percent (or less) of high school graduates, are primarily residential in nature, field (for the most part) Division I athletics teams, employ a high percentage of full-time tenured faculty, and fare well in the national rankings. The 23 campuses that constitute the California State University system are recognized as strong local and regional players (some with reputations that extend well beyond state boundaries), focusing primarily on baccalaureate and master's education with some doctoral and professional programs, providing access to a broad array of students, offering both full- and part-time opportunities, encouraging faculty to conduct research in areas of specific benefit to the surrounding community, and generally positioning themselves as drivers of success for the residents of the communities—and the communities themselves—in which those students reside. The 109 members of the California Community College system offer primarily lower-division classes and credentialing programs, are nonresidential, provide distributed and alternative learning systems for both adult and traditional students, and are widely regarded as a springboard into Cal State, UC, or private university alternatives. And the price points are similarly differentiated.

Surveys in California over the decades have underscored the success of this brand differentiation strategy. Residents know what UC, CSU, and CCC members stand for and what they focus on, and they know the relative value of the degrees they offer. They support, through tax policy, a higher per capita for members of the UC system than for members of the CSU or CCC systems (we could argue for hours about whether or not this is fair—but not whether it is true) because they believe them to be superior, following a more complex mission, and charged with a level of knowledge generation greater than that of their sister systems.

In the end, the value of the brand is determined by the consumer of the brand—the person to whom the brand provides that value. While this appears to be a tautology, it's also true. We all want to be proud of our own life narrative, of what we've been able to accomplish, and the best that alma mater can hope for is to play a hero's role in that individual story: This is where I became an adult. This is where I found myself. This is where I found my lifelong friends. This is where I found my mate. This is where I learned the skills that have taken me forward to where I am today. This is the place that made me who I am.

A Personal Brand Story

I was a California teenager when I made my college choice—back in the dark ages of academic marketing. I elected to go to UC Santa Cruz and was lucky enough to get accepted; at the time, it was the most difficult campus in the system to get into. It was small (fewer than 2,000 students), focused on undergraduate learning (highlighted by pass/fail grading), peculiar (residence halls hadn't been built, so we lived in trailers), and innovative (independent majors were encouraged). Plus, it was more than 500 miles from my natal home—an important consideration.

Now, draw the veil over my actual experience at UCSC and fast forward 10 to 15 years. Through the 1980s and into the 1990s, if people in a professional context asked where I'd gone to school, I'd frequently say "University of California" and let them fill in the blank. Why? In those years, the institutional reputation had gone from innovative to flaky, from peculiar to just plain stoned (helped along by the explosion of a growers' culture in the immediate area). It didn't seem to advance my professional cause—and, indeed, brought up questions I didn't want to answer about how I'd spent my undergraduate years—to specifically claim my Banana Slug roots.

Then, something interesting happened. UC Santa Cruz began to be known for its contribution to advancing knowledge in a number of areas. Charting DNA. Support for NASA missions. Oceanographic investigation and climate change. In fact, it came to claim a place among the "most productive" per capita institution in terms of faculty contribution to the discourse in science, the humanities, and social science. So I began to feel comfortable claiming it again, allowing it back into my personal narrative.

While the Banana Slug is not a heroic figure in my life narrative (or, perhaps, anybody's) I have come to value it for its own peculiar self—and what it contributed to the person I am today.

EXPRESSION

Once you understand the authentic value that your institution provides, it's time to develop materials—print, Web, or other—that clearly and effectively present the value of your brand to the target audience. This is the brand *expression*. (The process of creative development of the brand expression will be thoroughly covered in chapter 7, "Brand Activation.") And while you can develop and promote your brand expression in many ways, they all begin with one central, compound question: Who is your audience and what do you want them to do?

Now, the idea of differing brand approaches might seem contradictory to the context of a branding program in which all internal and external expressions must spring from a coherent central concept. But it's not. Whether the brand expression is hip and hot in order to appeal to prospective students, or more measured to explain the institution's status and plan to alumni, or sentimental and elegiac to support a planned gift initiative to aging alumni and parents, it should spring from a central understanding of the brand: its authenticity and value.

A useful adjunct to the development of the brand expression is a set of key messages, vetted for consistency with the brand and built upon provable assets and deliverables. Let's presume, for a moment, that you are a liberal arts college with a positioning as "fiercely committed to the undergraduate experience." Creative expressions of this platform have been tested with the target market—high-achieving students from a national pool—and achieved the desired response. Current students validate it as being true to their experience. Faculty and staff endorse it as being true to their understanding of the institution and a key part of why they remain loyal to its goals. Alumni and donors are reassured that the very characteristics they value—passion, quality, and commitment—are still fundamental to alma mater. Competitors are, ruefully and admittedly, far less fierce. So what does the key message platform look like?

For Prospective Students

"When it comes to your undergraduate experience, we walk the talk."

- We recruit the best, most engaged, most ambitious students.
  - Test scores, class rank, valedictorian/salutatorian
  - Student government, team, and club activities and leadership
- We have devoted ourselves to creating a challenging intellectual experience for all our students.
  - Full faculty in the classroom
  - Guided research experience starts first semester freshman year
  - Freshman seminars organized in residence halls
  - Annual spring symposium
  - Senior year capstone experience
- We're even better outside the classroom.
  - Intramural sports and other fitness opportunities
- We have world-class facilities.
  - Clubs, societies, and student leadership
  - Traditions and opportunities
  - Community service requirement
  - Architecture that encourages interaction
- We take you where you want to go.
  - Mandatory (integrated and supported) semester abroad
  - Great alumni network
  - "Lifetime" career services commitment

For Current Students

"Always remember, it *is* all about you."

- We listen and respond.
  - › Frequent out-of-class interaction between students and faculty
- NSSE data highlights.
  - › Student representation on board and key committees
  - › Faculty families in residence halls
- We want you to help shape your own experience.

Faculty and Staff

"When our students succeed, so do we."

- Teaching matters.
  - › Class load, office hour, and guided research expectations
  - › Student, as well as peer, evaluations considered in tenure review
- We are committed to stakeholder service.
  - › 24-hour deadline for response to inquiries
  - › Ongoing feedback/assessment methods

Alumni/ae

"The more things change, the more we stay the same."

- We pushed you further than you were prepared to go—and you liked it.
- You are part of us—and we a part of you—forever.
  - › Legacy admissions
  - › Career service involvement
  - › Alumni networking
- You, too, can continue to feel the energy.
  - › Giving
  - › Participating
  - › Challenging
  - › Continual learning

Such a key message platform—built to order for your institution—can guide communications planning, strategic orientation, editorial planning for the alumni magazine, the development of enrollment or capital campaign materials, and staff and faculty hiring decisions. It can also play a role—as it's discussed, analyzed, revised, and endorsed—in the development of another key issue in branding success: the development, orientation, and motivation of your best brand advocates.

AMBASSADORS

The wonderful and peculiar thing about brands is that everybody owns their own experience of them. Because of that, every individual who in some way represents the institution can either strengthen or weaken the brand by words or deeds. And because of their presumed "privileged" position and knowledge, faculty and students have the greatest influence on how the brand is perceived.

On the negative side are the faculty members who fatuously blog as holocaust-deniers, whose intemperate rants get caught and posted on YouTube, who can't keep their hands off students, who teach from dog-eared yellow-legal-pad notes older than the students in the room, or who otherwise soil themselves, dishonor the profession, and contribute to a high degree of cynicism about those institutions with which they are associated. Allied with them are the students who are caught cheating, who get hammered and barf in the neighbor's roses, who strip and paint themselves blue (or whatever the school's colors) at athletic contests (particularly if they are less-than-exemplary specimens of physicality), who get caught on film with Borat, who develop FaceBook or MySpace pages solely devoted to their beer bong prowess, or who resort to thuggery or gangsta behavior on national television.

But let's be positive. More often than not, faculty are earnest and hardworking members of society, committed to their students, their discipline, and to community service. They work late nights to ensure that their presentation of information captivates and encourages their students, they volunteer for causes and serve on nonprofit boards, they generate and advance ideas that change how we see the world and how progress is measured. Students in general take their work seriously and know that their college years are an important step in preparation for life after graduation. Even though there is only grudging acceptance of the academic freedom rationale behind tenure, many people do understand that faculty operate under other rules and can frequently get away with behavior that would get them fired in any other work environment. And barfing fraternity brothers? Well, we've all been part of that scene in one way or another—if not ourselves redepositing the results of our overly enthusiastic game of beer pong in the shrubbery, then holding the head of the poor slob who's doing so.

As brand ambassadors, faculty or students are more likely to muddy the picture because they simply don't understand the brand promise and can't, therefore, be the great institutional ambassadors they are both willing and qualified to be. Because a great faculty member—bright, articulate, on-message, committed, excited—is absolutely the best brand ambassador for your institution. Faculty are perceived to have first-hand knowledge: real, rather than programmed. Their role as the "interlocuters" between the institution and a key stakeholder group its serves—the students—is seen as being key to interpreting the success of the enterprise. All the research—from that conducted annually by the *Chronicle of Higher Education* to statewide and institution-specific surveys—shows that the public believes the primary purpose of colleges and universities, at least those they support through their tax dollars, is the education of the next generation.

The Integrated Marketing Core Committee

There was a time when a public relations professional never uttered the "m" word in front of faculty for fear of getting hammered with a high-brow lecture about how marketing is for toothpaste and cereal not higher education, and certainly not a liberal arts education.

Today, every premier college and university understands that competition for top students and faculty, for funding, and for recognition demands an effective and comprehensive program of marketing communications. The best schools recognize that the spirit and letter shaping such a program must come from deep within the institution, as well as from a realistic appraisal of what the "outside world" believes. At Trinity University, it was a well-appointed marketing committee that helped pull our campus across this threshold.

Trinity's Integrated Marketing Core Committee served as the guiding forum as the university developed its first-ever institution-wide marketing plan. Appointed by the president, the committee included senior-level faculty and administrators and received visible and ongoing support from the executive staff, a fact that empowered the committee's planning process from the start.

"Institutions change and evolve, and the IMCC's work offered Trinity an opportunity to reimagine itself in light of what we knew about it and what others thought about it," said Arturo Madrid, Murchison Distinguished Professor of Humanities and IMCC member. As an example, our research revealed that Texas was a negative factor among out-of-state prospects, but San Antonio was a strong positive. The IMCC determined that in our outreach beyond Texas, we'd play up San Antonio, but not necessarily Texas. "The individuals selected to the committee willingly engaged each other. As a result, ideas flowed and they were turned into actionable ways to tell the Trinity story in a compelling and consistent way," said Madrid.

Representing the interests and opinions of key constituencies, among them faculty, staff, students, and alumni, the committee's work included setting objectives for the plan, reviewing market research, and advising on the "fit" for Trinity of marketing directions and concepts. The committee's dialogue was robust and candid, but always respectful, as we set about the task of developing a positioning that represented the university's spirit and aspirations.

Chris Ellertson, dean of Trinity's admission and financial aid and IMCC member, said student recruitment was an immediate and direct beneficiary of the integrated marketing project. "We were able to explore what distinguishes Trinity, to learn more about our market position in the context of our enrollment goals, and how best to market Trinity to perspective students and parents," he said.

In April 2002, the committee delivered a 70-page marketing plan to the university president that has served as a blueprint for how Trinity would move forward to meet its overall marketing and communications objectives. The committee's work ensured that the plan would be embraced by the university community because it reflected a deep and detailed investigation that included input from all Trinity's constituencies, as well as counsel from experts in the field of higher education marketing.

The Integrated Marketing Core Committee met monthly during the development of the marketing plan and launched several ad hoc task groups. The committee continues to meet to discuss new communication initiatives, concepts, and directions. Although offered an opportunity to rotate off the committee, no IMCC member has done so, choosing instead to continue the good work of reaching out to new audiences who may not yet know enough about our exceptional institution.

Sharon Jones Schweitzer
Assistant Vice President for University Communications
Trinity University

How, then, do you make these smart, demanding, and market-wary people (who, of course, think otherwise) into your best brand ambassadors? It starts with intentionality—recognition that they are key to the success of your brand initiative—and requires continuing involvement. Assembling a branding initiative team is imperative, including representatives of the enrollment management team, student life, communications, advancement and alumni relations, athletics, physical plant, administrative support, student leadership, and faculty—any group with direct access to and responsibility for stakeholder relations. The team should meet early in the process to help set goals for the branding project, review the research methodology and materials, participate in the analysis of data, discuss positioning, review key messages, advocate for the adoption and implementation of the brand marketing plan. And be careful: Don't stack the committee with folks who are already known to be on your side. That tactic will make your recommendations and results suspect in the broader academic community. It's a great idea to include some known contrarians on the committee; their voices will be critical in developing strategies for communicating the brand plan to campus audiences, and their endorsement will carry with it the imprimatur of their known opposition to the very idea of brand marketing.

The road to Damascus (OK, San Antonio ...)

In 1999, when we began a major market positioning project with Trinity University in San Antonio, one of the faculty members of our integrated marketing committee was a chemistry professor named Nancy Mills. Initially, Mills was on the committee because she was deeply skeptical of its intention, fearing that the marketing effort would result in strengthening the professional programs to the detriment of the arts and sciences. She was determined to stop such an effort in its tracks. We welcomed her to the team because we knew that if we could change her mind, her initial skepticism would make her an even stronger advocate for the program.

Through a process of data generation, analysis, positioning exploration, and plan development, Mills became such an advocate for the branding and marketing effort that she took it upon herself to sit down individually with every department chair in the university and explain why and how they should be involved. She became, in the process, a great brand ambassador.

STORYTELLING

Early on, I asserted that the best brands become stories—enduring narratives that twist themselves into our collective consciousness. But this assertion triggers questions: Really? Why? And, what makes a good story? And, even more important, how can you find and refine your own institution's brand stories?

For the "why," let's turn to both history and biochemistry. Deep in our human past, huddled around the fire at the entrance to the cave, our ancestors sought to make sense of the world—to transmit what they knew of it or were learning of it—through the simple device of storytelling: recounting the narrative of events that they had experienced. If Og got eaten by a saber-toothed tiger, and Ug had watched it happen, the story would in all likelihood either glorify or diminish Og—depending on the lesson that the teller wanted to transmit—and would contain some key elements, such as "don't go near that saber-toothed tiger" or "sneak up on him from behind with a really sharp spear." Absent written language, oral recitation—and the occasional cave painting—was the only way that humans could compile any sense of the world larger than their own direct experience. This ability, in fact, led paleontologist Stephen Jay Gould to define man as "the primate who tells stories"[2]— not "the primate who walks upright" or "the primate who knows how to steam milk for a double latte." Whole, complex societies were built around the oral tradition, and the Homeric legacy—in which can be found many of the most abiding, archetypal myths and images of Western civilization—is based on both a mnemonic and narrative structure that has passed down to us through the ages.

But it's not just tradition, or tradition as an extraneous overlay. According to Richard Maxwell and Robert Dickman, "Storytelling is innate in the human psyche ... so hardwired into us that it has its own place on our genome—a gene called FOXP2 ... the first of what scientists believe is a whole constellation of genes that make language and narrative possible. ... From a cellular level on up, we are all born storytellers."[3] Numerous experiments on cognitive psychology from kindergarten up to creative leadership in advertising agencies (though perhaps, upon reflection, this is not as well-diversified a set of respondents as we might wish) have shown that memory is enhanced and opinion swayed when we go beyond "just the facts, ma'am" to delivering those facts in a story context. A whole field of storytelling *in an organizational context* has sprung up in recent years, moving the impact of storytelling out of the personal and into the business and professional realm. "People don't want more information," writes Annette Simmons. "They are up to their eyeballs in information. They want *faith*—faith in you, your goals, your success, in the story you tell. It is faith that moves mountains, not facts. Facts do not give birth to faith. Faith needs a story to sustain it—a *meaningful* story that inspires belief in you and renews hope that your ideas indeed offer what you promise. ... Story is your path to creating faith."[4]

So the questions evolve: What makes a good story? and What makes a good *brand* story?

For direction on what makes a good story, turn to Andy Goodman, a former Hollywood screenwriter and the story guru whom Al Gore tapped when he wanted to train 1,000 avid global warriors on how to make effective presentations of his *An Inconvenient Truth*. Goodman offers the Ten Immutable Laws of Storytelling:

1. Stories are about people.

2. The people in your story have to want something.

3. Stories need to be fixed in time and space.

4. Let your characters speak for themselves.

5. Audiences bore easily.

6. Stories speak the audience's language.

7. Stories stir up emotions.

8. Stories don't tell: they show.

9. Stories have at least one "moment of truth."

10. Stories have clear meaning.[5]

But how to link these "laws" in a compelling brand story? In Maxwell and Dickman's formulation, "a story is a fact, wrapped in an emotion that compels us to take an action that transforms our world."[6] And all too often, colleges and universities fall into the trap of parading their brand "features"—facts and statistics—as if those data in some way tell the story of the institution. But facts alone don't tell the story, and frequently they are interpreted in an entirely surprising way.

Some years past, Lipman Hearne conducted a major research project for the Annapolis Group, a consortium of leading liberal arts colleges. We held a dozen focus groups in four cities around the country to find out what the parents of high-achieving, college-bound teens knew about liberal arts colleges, who they thought would benefit from attending such an institution, and what the likely outcome of such an education would be. All participants held baccalaureate or advanced degrees from major research or comprehensive universities and had no direct experience with liberal arts colleges. In addition to probing awareness and understanding of the overall category, we also asked questions about key features that the liberal arts colleges had been touting, such as small classes.

At our first session in Boston, a handful of Annapolis Group presidents were in attendance behind the one-way glass. Our moderator had just asked the question "What comes to mind when you hear the term *small classes*?" as a salt-and-pepper-haired, distinguished college president popped a yellow peanut M&M into his mouth. A dark-haired, intense woman leaned forward and, without a pause, said, "Small classes? Bad professors." A sudden intake of collective breath behind the glass almost caused our president to choke and others to leap to pound on his back, which, fortunately, succeeded in dislodging the offending M&M before we were called on to execute the Heimlich maneuver. In the back-room ruckus, we nearly missed her rationale—which, from her perspective, made perfect sense. At her large public research university, the good professors had standing-room-only classes, with lines of students snaking down the hall hoping to get admitted. Word-of-mouth marketing had clearly defined both good professors and bad, and everybody avoided the latter. Hence, small classes meant awful classes. And this woman wasn't the only one who held this impression: At every focus group we held, one or two or a few participants had an equivalent response.[7]

Now, I tell this story for two reasons. When I include it in a presentation to groups, I do so to emphasize the importance of moving beyond *features*—small classes—to *benefits*: intense interaction between students and faculty, dialogue among students, personalized and transformative knowledge-sharing, no student left behind, etc. And I like to hear them gasp in horror when they learn that their target market has been known to draw the exact opposite conclusion from what they are trying to communicate when they parade their proud statistics and features.

And the other reason I tell the story is to encourage people to start thinking about their own brand stories. How can the feature of "small classes" (if that's a key differentiator for your institution) be better illustrated by stories than by a boast that "our student/faculty ratio is 11/1"? What are those compelling stories that encapsulate just how your institution delivers on particular aspects of its brand promise? How do you find those aspects of your organization that are truly differentiating, and collect stories that relate to them?

For answers, read on.

---

1. For any reader who cannot figure out what the asterisks stand for, please put one dollar in an envelope along with the signed title to your car, and mail it to me. Please enclose SASE for prompt response (and clean out the glove compartment).

2. Robyn M. Dawes, "A Message from Psychologists to Economists: Mere Predictability Doesn't Matter Like It Should (Without a Good Story Appended to It)," *Journal of Economic Behavior and Organization* 39 (May 1999): 29–40.

3. Richard Maxwell and Robert Dickman, *The Elements of Persuasion: Use Storytelling to Pitch Better, Sell Faster, and Win More Business* (New York: HarperCollins, 2007), 4.

4. Annette Simmons, *The Story Factor: Inspiration, Influence, and Persuasion Through the Art of Storytelling* (Cambridge, MA: Basic Books, 2006), 3.

5. Andy Goodman, *Storytelling as Best Practice*, 4th ed. (Los Angeles: A. Goodman, 2008), 38–39.

6. Maxwell and Dickman, *Elements of Persuasion*, 5.

7. As a storyteller, I must confess: this is a composite presentation based, in fact, on what actually happened. The actual scenario wasn't perhaps as dramatic—the president was able to hack the M&M out of his throat without assistance, for example—but the "bad professors" response is absolutely true. As to the color of the M&M ...

CHAPTER 5

BRAND PLATFORM

GOOGLE "BRAND." At today's writing, 911,000,000 hits.

"Branding": 50,500,000 hits.

"Brand strategy": 1,200,000.

"Brand experience": 893,000.

"Brand map": 37,300.

"Brand platform": 33,100.

In other words, a lot of folks out there are talking about branding in its many forms, using language that is at times harmonious and at other times conflicting. Early on, we adopted the working definition of a *brand* as a "promise of an experience"—ultimately delivered as a narrative that has the power to grip the stakeholder's imagination. We explored the how and what of differentiation—how your brand stands out from the crowd. And we've looked at the various characteristics that a strong brand must have: authenticity, value, materials that express the core of the experience, supporting stories. But how do you actually build out the brand so that it connects with the core values of your institution, so you can have some sort of filter or guide by which to evaluate the ongoing presentation and expression of the brand?

The answer: You construct a rubric of some sort, a heuristic device that captures all the elements of your brand in a fashion that makes it possible to display, discuss, and remember the brand formulation. The shape that rubric takes—whether a pyramid, a blueprint, a polygon, or any other form that firms construct to create a proprietary brand model—is unimportant. A map suggests a path and a journey; a platform, something to build upon; a pyramid, a hierarchy; a continuum, an ongoing sequence; a blueprint, a bespoke construct. These are all evocative and accurate representations of how to think about a brand. But you know what? None of it matters, as long as the form captures the necessary elements and the picture tells the story. I have chosen to describe our model as a platform because it suggests that the distilled framework is not the whole brand—it's the framework or the stage on which the brand operates. The goal is not to build the platform and stop there; the goal is for the platform to become a means by which the full brand is lived. So the task, then, is to understand the platform—its inherent character and potential—and develop its characteristics and attributes in such a way that the brand can be valued, understood, and expressed in a meaningful way by your brand ambassadors.

And let's face it, sometimes an illustration is worth a chapter full of words.

In our formulation, any higher education brand contains six incremental elements:[1]

- Mission: the fundamental focus of the institution

- Positioning: a clear understanding of where we stand relative to our competitors and to our audience's knowledge and expectations

- Proof: the verifiable assets and attributes that enable us to claim that positioning

- Pledge: the sustaining beliefs and values that motivate us

- Personality: the face we show the world

- Payoff: the reward that our stakeholders derive from their affiliation

And smack-dab in the middle of them is the Big Idea: the essence or "driver" of the brand, a short-hand answer to the question What is this brand all about? In this structure, *mission* is fundamental; *positioning* and *proofs* are functional; and *Big Idea* and *pledge* are strategic, defining the focus and direction of the brand. *Personality* and *payoff* are emotional—creating and occupying the zone where the brand truly comes into its own. (For a visual representation of the brand platform, see pages 68–71.)

There are many ways to develop a mnemonic structure for the brand, and such a structure should not be seen as the culmination—the end-all, be-all—of the branding process. Capturing the brand in visual form often makes explanation, adoption, and activation more possible, and it allows for ongoing reflection as the institution attempts to "live the brand." But before we get to the visuals, let's explore the elements more fully.

MISSION

Fundamental to all aspects of the brand is your institutional mission. Remember: Marketing that doesn't advance your mission is irrelevant and wrong. This is both true and a useful inoculation against the skeptics in academe who insist on seeing marketing and/or branding as shallow, suspect, and essentially devious promotions reminiscent of *National Lampoon*'s infamous 1973 cover that warned, "If you don't buy this magazine, we'll kill this dog." The marketing and advertising professions—in their popular representations from *The Man in the Grey Flannel Suit* to AMC's *Mad Men*—are assumed to be populated by crass, cynical, and grasping spin artists whose primary motivation is how to quickly and profitably "put lipstick on the pig."[2] And while this may be true in some cases, the people who are successful in marketing, public relations, and branding work in academe recognize that *authenticity* (again, that word) is fundamental to brand's appeal.

Service brands—such as those of colleges, universities, and preparatory schools—are experiential in nature. They are not products that can be resized, given a new label, attached to a celebrity spokesperson, and given a temporary boost in market share powered by legions of impulse buyers. They are lived brands, and as such they are dependent on the ability of the institution to deliver on the promise—coherently, over time, in the real world. In this way they are more like hotels and health clubs, resorts and restaurants, conference centers and concert halls, cities and synagogues, than they are like packaged goods or consumer products.

Experiential brands are about enacting the values that stakeholders attribute to the organization. Brand communications are the gateway to a relationship that, properly managed, can sustain the exchange of mutual benefit for both the institution and the stakeholder for decades. Successful higher ed brands are fundamentally based in the mission. Are you a community college, dedicated to access, teaching, low-cost provision of important academic services, and responsiveness to the community? Then your mission should state so, explicitly. Are you a K–12 preparatory school devoted to academic quality, moral development, and religious formulation? Then your mission statement should make that clear. Are you a public research university, operating to fulfill the classic mission of research, education, and service? Then your mission statement has to stand on all three legs of the tripartite stool.

Your *mission statement*—or a pertinent nugget of it—is, therefore, the foundation of your brand platform. Its visible presence will go a long way toward reassuring the skeptics that your branding initiative is focused on achieving goals that they endorse, and it will act as a visible reminder to all involved in the effort that, in the end, it's not all about ads or taglines or clever guerrilla tactics (though, well done, these can help hugely); it's about fulfilling the institutional mission.

POSITIONING

In chapter 3, our discussion of positioning covered the core elements: institutional capacity and vision, competitive context, and marketplace perception. But obviously there's not room for a long series of statements or validating details in this small space in the brand platform. One simple and common place to start is by completing the following statement:

> More than any other institution, (*institution name here*) is better able to (*distinct, verifiable action/impact here*) for (*target audience here*).

Now this looks impossibly clunky when delivered as a template, so let's fill in possible positioning statements for well-known academic brands and see how it works.

> More than any other institution, Harvard provides an unparalleled opportunity for very bright, ambitious students to experience a legacy of achievement.

Okay, maybe that was too easy—or too reliant on the Harvard name. Let's try another:

> More than any competing institution, Northern Arizona University offers greater personal attention to students who want an unconventional experience through faculty who are focused on teaching.

The key in that example is that competing institutions in the public university context in Arizona tend to be much larger research universities that have a more difficult time delivering on the "personal attention" aspect for undergraduate students.

The form of the positioning statement can change, as long as the relative competitive advantage still stands clear.

> More than any other institution, Trinity University combines the best elements of a residential college with the range of liberal and professional programs of a large urban university for students who are focused on personal and professional achievement.

I admit that nobody is going to be singing that statement as the curtain rises, but it does start to provide a framework for thinking about differentiation and market positioning. In Trinity's case, the key words and phrases are achievement (Trinity students are very ambitious), *urban/ residential* (one of Trinity's differentiators is its location in San Antonio), and *liberal and professional programs* (for a school of 2,400 students, Trinity offers an unparalleled array of business, engineering, education, social sciences, arts, and humanities courses).

PROOFS

Climbing higher in the platform, proofs are the validating points—the evidence that the positioning statement is supportable. Proofs are definitive and verifiable; they are demonstrable assets of the brand, attributes that are indisputable, measurable, and inherent to the institution. They are not wishful thinking, how you hope to be regarded by your target market. They are the underpinnings of how you actually deliver on your brand promise. They provide a means by which you can keep track—regularly and quantifiably—of the quality of your services and your institutional ability to continue to keep its competitive edge. Knowing these attributes—these proofs—helps in the budgeting and planning process: If you know what's important to maintaining the vitality of your brand, you'll know where you need to invest in faculty and staff, programs, and facilities. They also provide an important asset in your internal marketing. Showing faculty, in particular, how the measurable attributes are an inherent part of the brand reassures them about the authenticity and granularity of the branding process: It's not just surface noise, it's deep in your institutional DNA.

Provable, measurable attributes for various institutional categories might include these:

- **For research universities:** level of federal research funding (and/or rate of growth of such funding); level of corporate/foundation support; range of majors; rankings of schools, colleges, and professional programs; SAT/ACT of incoming students; retention and graduation rates; percentage of students receiving financial aid; average household income of students; alumni giving percentage

- **For comprehensive universities:** range of majors; SAT/ACT of incoming students; retention and graduation rates; percentage of classes taught by full-time faculty; percentage of students receiving financial aid; percentage of classes with fewer than 25 students; average household income of students; alumni giving percentage

- **For liberal arts colleges:** SAT/ACT of incoming students; retention and graduation rates; percentage of students receiving financial aid; percentage of classes with fewer than 25 students; student/faculty ratio; alumni giving percentage

- **For community colleges:** number of degree/certificate programs; percentage of teachers holding terminal degrees; availability of classes online/off time; relationship to and involvement with community leaders

- **For preparatory schools:** size of classes; range of athletic/scholarly opportunities; percentage of teachers holding terminal degrees; percentage of students receiving financial aid; percentage of graduates attending college or university; "honor roll" of colleges that graduates attend

While these category attributes are a good start, other, more specific proofs that are aligned with your distinct, differentiated market position would also have to be developed, and a built-out brand platform would include a means to assess each attribute in terms of its current expression and how success would be measured in the future, as in the example in table 1 derived from the attribute chart of a leading national university.

Table 1. Attribute Chart of Leading National University

Proof	Way Lived/Expressed	Measurement of Success
Interdisciplinary innovation	• Variety of interdisciplinary courses each term • Ability to design interdisciplinary major • Ease of taking courses that are not within major • Number of team-taught courses	• Percentage of students participating in interdisciplinary courses • Percentage of students with double major
Best-in-class research opportunities	• Grant money available to support student research projects • Faculty incentives for mentoring students in research endeavors • Summer research program for entering students	• Amount of grant money available for student research projects as compared to other universities in same category

With performance charts such as this constructed around each of your key brand attributes, you will be able to both track the activities that differentiate your institution and guarantee its ability to "walk the talk" in a way that fulfills your stakeholders' expectations. And that's an important step into the next level of the brand platform, where the fundamentals that are the basis of the brand are distilled into one clear, directional summary statement.

Strategic Brand Development for Enterprise Universities

Not all higher ed institutions are tuition- or enrollment-driven. While their core mission remains education, enterprise universities are much more: knowledge generators, economic engines, community developers, research partners, and often national and global ambassadors. Corporate and federal research funds, state support, foundation grants, technology transfer, athletics and other auxiliary businesses are critically important to enterprise universities, and their audiences have correspondingly diverse reasons for investing and believing in the institution's brand. Undergraduate appeal can be a key factor in the "buzz," but it won't establish the brand's universal value. Instead, successful branding demands a sticky Big Idea that goes far beyond marketing and messaging and enables the enterprise university to relate to diverse audiences in terms that directly relate to their own needs and perspectives.

The most effective of these universities, no matter how complex, have big ideas at the core. Think of Cal Berkeley's radical genius, or the University of Michigan "Powerhouse" (winning in all things). MIT is consistently the first mover on the premise that technological mastery should focus on sharing knowledge that transforms society (through its open-courseware initiative, for example); call it the world's idea mainframe.

Brand development for the enterprise university must follow two paths. One is to foster "badge" membership that everyone who affiliates owns as part of his or her representation of self, regardless of "point of entry." (In this way, the retired business owner who consumes MIT's political science knowledge online is as much an "MIT person" as is the graduating Rhodes Scholar.) The second is to infuse a vast array of activities with a singular characteristic reason for doing that nurtures an almost intuitive understanding of the university's claim. When the University of Chicago creates charter schools on the city's South Side, for example, it makes sense because of the university's mission of democratizing inquiry and academic rigor. In this initiative, Chicago is not just talking, it is doing—and the brand impact is much greater.

So what are some special considerations in branding for enterprise universities?

- **Internal vision-setting must recognize the voices of many chiefs.** Rampant internal entrepreneurialism—one of the forces behind successful enterprise universities—also makes these institutions highly decentralized in decision-making. Gaining sign-off by a dozen deans and unit CEOs may be exhausting, but it is critical.

- **Market research must be truly multiconstituent.** The brand cannot be built on student or alumni input alone (even if enrollment or alumni fundraising is an immediate priority). Parallel research investigations must work together to surface a brand premise that rises to the level of representing the shared ground between constituents with very different entry portals.

- **Research excellence and importance are givens in the category (just as student-centered education is indigenous to liberal arts colleges).** Major public universities often make the mistake of promoting research status—an in-state point of distinction—in the national or global context where it is a universal baseline. An enterprise university must stake a claim beyond research excellence to a clear point of value: why the country and the world, and not just students or the state, should pay attention.

- **The defining conversations matter.** Many enterprise universities are choosing to leverage big-issue themes in which they can make distinctive contributions that matter worldwide. Such themes, such as global health, the environment, the development of cosmopolitan cities, and new models for citizen learning, cross

boundaries not only of nations but also between business and academia, between research and the public interest, between the collective good and the personal aspirations of scholars and students.

Finally, enterprise university brands—like all others—must speak to the heart and not just the head.

Joselyn Zivin
Senior Vice President
Lipman Hearne

THE BIG IDEA

We have a rule about the Big Idea: five words or less. Otherwise, you run the danger of simply repeating the mission or positioning statement. Remember, the Big Idea offers a short-hand answer to the question What is this brand all about? It is a succinct sound bite that resonates throughout the brand structure, striking a chord with the mission, positioning, proofs, pledge, personality, and payoff.

Let's look at a handful of "brand essence" statements from a set of universities. Rather than having you see if you can match the statement with the institution, ask yourself these questions: What does this statement say about the institution? Does it match what I know—or think I know—about the place? Does it make me want to learn more or get further engaged?

1. Arizona State University is a vanguard.

2. University of Denver ... a great private university dedicated to the public good.

3. Concordia University Montreal: Engage. Commit. Challenge.

4. University of Ontario Institute of Technology. Challenge. Innovate. Connect.

5. University of Idaho: An intellectually energized, intimate college environment.

6. University of Windsor: Taking responsibility for the future.

7. Northwestern University: Innovative teaching and pioneering research in a highly collaborative environment.

8. Stetson University: Shared commitment to educate students to lead great lives.

Okay, so some of them violate our five-word maximum. And some of them are relatively hard to distinguish from each other (suggesting some confusion between a tagline developed for public consumption and a brand essence that distills the institutional understanding of its role and its character).[3] But for the ones that really work—ASU and Denver and Idaho—you can get a real sense of the institution at its core: what it values, how it acts, how it wants you to relate to it. So the essence holds up a mirror to a certain kind of person and says: "Recognize yourself? If you do, this is the place for you to make your mark."

Finding the Big Idea, like brainstorming, is equal parts science and art—and a good copy-editor's slashing red pencil cutting out the flotsam and filler to get to the delicious, nutty core. While it may seem a sophism to say it, a Big Idea has to actually be big and it has to have an idea as its core. It acts as a strategic driver, a fundamental understanding by which the organization makes decisions critical to its future. It doesn't change from season to season and doesn't necessarily get expressed as direct-to-market language, but it stands as a touchstone for all brand communications.

PLEDGE

This is the place where some branding tomes get kind of creepy. They start talking about the brand as if it were sentient, as if it actually had and was able to act on its intentionality: "the brand values honesty"; "the brand feels committed"; "the brand wants to conquer the world"; "the brand has to go home and take a cold shower."

In fact, the brand is our construct, how we each regard the specific institution or service or product in relation to similar or competing institutions, services, or products. It feels nothing and thinks nothing. It does, however, have to be guided by underlying principles—core values—that everybody who participates in brand formulation and execution can both agree with and take to heart. This is particularly important in experiential brands—brands that are lived every day by people interacting withone another through the brand. So another way of thinking about intentionality or direction in the brand is as the answers to fundamental, "felt" questions. How do the people who live the brand act? What do they believe? What guides their decisions and actions in the institutional context? What is the pledge that we make to our stakeholders?

We can think about the pledge as *the direction the brand is moving:* how the people who live the brand act as they make decisions about the institutional presence and future, how they define the principles by which they operate, how they intend to deliver on the promise that they make.

These principles will be largely determined by a handful of related factors: institutional governance, mission, and strategic intent.

Governance

A public institution will have a very different governance structure than an institution that is part of a religious or denominational organization. Although I realize that, for many alumni, "Buckeye" or "Gator" or "Tarheel" is their religion—services held every game day with hourly sacraments on ESPN—the operating principles of the organization are going to be dictated in part by what the actual governance structure permits or demands. An institution formulated in and governed by a faith community will have key language from that faith community among its operating principles; by law, a public institution could not use that same language.

Mission

Institutional mission—including reference to access, quality, outreach, preparation for life, community service, or other aspirations—will also determine intentionality. In some cases, mission is so fundamental as to be top-of-mind for every stakeholder. At the United States Military Academy, any resident of "beast barracks" could shout out "Duty. Honor. Country." if asked about West Point principles; if they couldn't, expect them to drop and give you 20 times 20. At Wheaton College in Illinois, "Christ-centered" would be the first words out of anybody's mouth. In many cases, the mission-based principles are going to be more nebulous—but they must be identified, nevertheless.

Strategic Intent

The strategic plan, as an evolving blueprint for how the institution will achieve its mission, can and will also contribute to how the brand is lived and how it evolves. Obviously aligned with the mission, the strategic plan might require occasional adjustments in the principles as the institution focuses its intention and resources to meet its goals: greater emphasis on improving the student profile, or investing more in faculty research, or getting more involved in the community would all require recognition as part of brand intent.

Clearly articulating the principles on which the institution operates—the commitment it makes to its stakeholders—will carry benefits beyond the development of the brand platform. It plays a part in strategy development, hiring decisions, program review and assessment, and other mission-critical processes.

In the nonprofit context, the pledge tends to be focused on community benefit, which is defined as the value it delivers to the stakeholders it serves. Aligned with your institutional strategic plan, the pledge may well include some sort of direct return to your stakeholders from your ability to achieve your institutional mission. It is in some ways "categorical"; that is, other institutions with a similar mission or governance (public versus private, for example, or research versus liberal arts) may well have a very similar thrust. But it is further sharpened by your differentiating aspects, your USP.

The pledge often frames your community relations and local or regional press relations efforts. Typically, it's expressed as a "we" statement: "We believe ideas make a difference"; "We develop well-rounded people"; "We believe anything is possible." It may well be prominent in your president's speeches to civic and business groups and will be buttressed by data as well as stories: the number of students doing volunteer work, and a particular student who launched an afterschool mentoring program; access provided by opportunity grants and scholarships, and a particular alumnae who is the first in her family to graduate from college and sponsored a scholarship after she was part of a successful IPO; the dollar volume of sponsored research, and the story of the corporate-university partnership that developed a new dry-cleaning technology that is making big bucks for the institution while cleaning up the environment. It remains, however, an institutional presentation, rather than a more intensely individual one. To achieve the latter—and for the potential to unleash the passionate, personal aspects of the brand—you have to move into the next level, where the emotional impact is clarified and felt.

PERSONALITY

Understanding brand *personality* as an emotional expression of the brand is crucial to the creative process, in particular. It's at the emotional level that brands are lived and felt, where they stake their claim to enduring relationships with the people who affiliate with them.

Brand personality captures how the brand comes across, how it sounds, feels, tastes, and (maybe) smells. In the corporate world, the Wal-Mart brand personality would include "friendly" (why else the personal greeters by every door?), Nordstrom would include "helpful" ("that's all right, I'm just looking around"), Pepsi would (hopefully, after all they've spent on "the Pepsi generation") read "youthful," and Apple would be "hip" or "innovative." Each institution, by its history, communications, and actions, has a personality. Even if it doesn't seem to, the personality is probably there, but as an undefined or unexplored milquetoast.

Institutional personalities affect our perception of the institutions. And institutional personality influences both the nature of the people who want to be involved with the institution and the satisfaction they will derive from that involvement. We always say that enrollment materials—a primary expression of the brand—should act not as a window into the institution but as a mirror in which the observer can see himself or herself. And the reflection in the mirror for the student who would do best at Caltech is very different from the reflection for the student who would only be happy at Harvard or Amherst or "Go Blue" Michigan. And the further you get from the very top of the "best of the best" pyramid, the more important that personality becomes.

Personality is discovered through a process of internal intake—the enthusiasm or lack thereof of stakeholders, the energy and passion and character of faculty and students—coupled with external research. While you don't necessarily want to go all Baba Wawa in the process ("If you were a tree, what kind of tree would you be?"), it can be helpful to think of an institutional personality in terms of archetype. Is it more masculine or more feminine? Demure or forthright? Formal or unbuttoned? Clean-shaven or hirsute? What actor would play the role—in what play?

Exploring the personality in this way is both amusing and productive. While the answer is not "Jimmy Stewart in MacBeth" (or we hope it's not), such an exercise can clarify the embedded presumptions about the brand personality.

PAYOFF

Emotional attachment creates and sustains brand loyalty and nurtures the continuing relationship between student and graduate and the institution that is essential in academe. Affiliation with a strong and beloved brand creates a distinct and valued payoff for the individual—a payoff that, properly nurtured, can evolve and accrete new dimensions to last a lifetime.

So what is the payoff, and how can it be expressed?

Put simply, the payoff is the benefit of belonging, what the individual derives from involvement with the brand. It is intensely personal: the foundation of the lifecycle relationship between alumnus/ae and institution, the passion that motivates friends and supporters, the spice in the goulash, the "this is me" slogan on the plain white T, the *alma* in alma mater.

Payoff statements typically are framed as first-person declarations:

"I've found my tribe."

"I feel connected and able to achieve."

"I matter."

"I'm different—and glad of it."

"I deserve—and got—the best."

Isolating this payoff is central to the development of constituent communications, whether you're addressing prospective students, current students, faculty and staff, alumni and donors, or friends and supporters from the broader community. The emotional impact is great; it represents the primary motivation that interests prospects in you, motivates them as they experience your institution, and fires their passion as they build a long-term, mutually beneficial relationship with you.

The individual payoff can only be determined through research, probably qualitative. It's not what you want them to value and appreciate about their relationship with you, it's what they actually do value and welcome about that relationship, how they define it. It's not "institution speak," it's "I feel." And you can't invent this yourself in a way that will resound authentically. You can aggregate, condense, refine, and polish, but you can't invent it whole cloth. It just won't feel or sound real.

But don't forget: The payoff also has to sound right to you, an ambassador for your institution. Your experience informs and resonates with the benefit you deliver; you should be able to say, "Yes, I feel that way, too" in terms of your role at the institution and how you serve the mission. If you're out of sync with the brand payoff, or the faculty and staff at the institution dismiss it as irrelevant, you probably haven't pinned it down in precise and meaningful language. So just keep trying until you get it right.

BRAND PLATFORM USE AND EXAMPLES

It's important to note that the brand platform is only a heuristic to capture and portray the complex elements of the brand. It's not an end in itself. It's not the philosopher's stone that will turn dross into gold. But it is a very useful way to categorize the elements of the brand, to remind yourself of its functional, strategic, and emotional aspects, and then guide your process of brand expression.

The empty brand platform, developed and used by Lipman Hearne, looks like this:

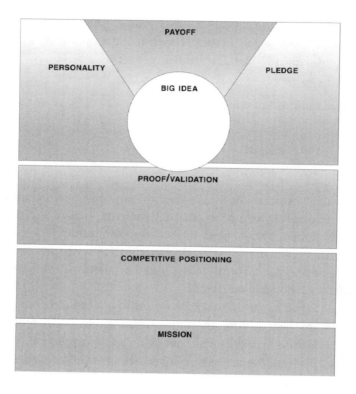

You'll note that the elements are grouped so that "types" of information are put together. *Mission*, *positioning*, and *proofs* are all fundamental, functional, and provable characteristics of the brand, less subject to interpretation, more quantitative than qualitative. The *Big Idea* and our *pledge* move into the strategic—the catalytic, organizing principles that command our attention and motivate us to act in the best interests of the brand and the community it serves. And *personality* and *payoff* are emotional, touching the heart in a way that proofs and mission never will.

For illustration, see the brand platforms below, specific characteristics of which have been redacted so as not to give away trade secrets.

This first brand platform is for a public institution in the American West with an access mission.

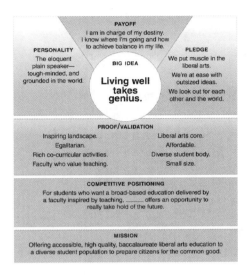

For another institution—an urban university with a strong co-op program and a history of applied research—the platform contains the same elements with very different specifics.

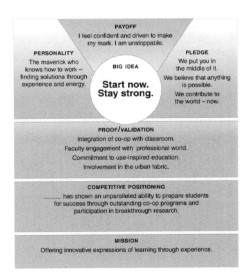

For a major international research university, a history of scholarship and service provides the basis for an ambitious brand expression.

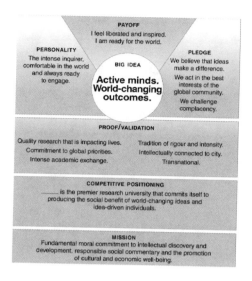

For an institution focused on engineering education, the brand platform reinforces the "quant-jock" sense of technical proficiency.

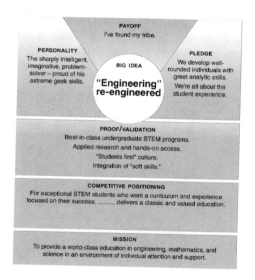

For a private undergraduate college, working hard to distinguish itself in a competitive context of the crowded Northeast, "personality" differentiation becomes ever more important.

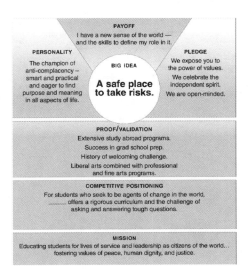

For a Midwest regional public university that needed to define itself in the competitive set of sister institutions in the same system, the students themselves really expressed the key elements of the brand platform.

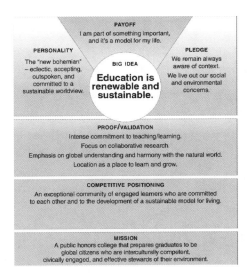

And from the brand platform, aligned with the goals of the branding initiative, springs the brand marketing plan. Read on!

---

1. This model is the result of a long process of exploration and definition led by Ken G. Kabira, Joselyn Zivin, Libby Morse, and Laura Ress at Lipman Hearne.

2. Credited to securities analyst Henry Blodget.

3. Derrick Daye and Brad VanAuken at BrandingStrategyInsider.com differentiate between *brand essence* and *tagline* by referring to corporate examples. Nike essence: Authentic Athletic Performance. Nike tag: Just do it. Hallmark essence: Caring Shared. Hallmark tag: When you care enough to send the very best. Jan. 13, 2008.

CHAPTER 6

DISSEMINATING YOUR BRAND

AS WITH ANY MARKETING CHALLENGE, the first issues to address in terms of brand marketing are *audience* and *intent*. These are closely followed by *resource commitment*. For major international consumer products corporations, the resource commitment issue is less intense. Procter & Gamble or Microsoft, for example, can "flood the zone" with segmented, focused advertising. In fact, the P&G house of brands spent $2.62 billion on advertising in 2007[1]—perhaps reinforcing the old CEO lament, "I know that half of our advertising isn't working, I just don't know which half!" (though in these days of click-throughs and keywords, knowing what's working becomes more clear every day).

But for institutions in the higher education sphere, resource availability is a very different matter. A for-profit, marketing-focused institution such as the University of Phoenix can and does commit as much as 25 percent of its gross revenue to marketing activities, including Internet marketing, direct mail, print and broadcast advertising, television advertising, naming rights, re-marketing, and referrals. In 2007 alone, this totaled nearly $660 million committed to "selling and promotional" activities.[2] And it worked. Degreed enrollments grew from 205,100 in 2003 to 313,700 in 2007—an increase of nearly 65 percent.[3] In 2008, enrollment skyrocketed again. Career Education Corporation, a for-profit entity that operates more than 80 campuses for 90,000 students throughout the United States, the U.K., Canada, France, and the United Arab Emirates, dedicates nearly 28 percent of its total revenue to advertising and admissions expense. (See sidebar interview with Gary McCullough, Career Ed CEO, in chapter 1.)

Marketing surveys conducted by Lipman Hearne over the past decade show that nonprofit institutional resource commitment on marketing activities is—no surprise—much, much lower. The average expenditure for marketing and communications activities among public colleges and universities (not counting salaries, benefits, and embedded costs) comes in at just below 1 percent of the operating budget; in private institutions, more dependent on tuition revenue, the number rises to a far-from-robust 1.6 percent.[4] Deeper on-campus drill-downs through comprehensive marketing and communications inventories reveal that 4 to 8 percent of the overall institutional budget is expended on these activities when salaries, benefits, and widely decentralized expenditures (such as those made by athletics, event, continuing education, and alumni relations departments) are taken into account. After conducting such a comprehensive inventory, we can frequently trigger a very effective process of coordinating marketing activities by asking the president or chancellor, "Is there anything else on which you're spending an equivalent amount that is not operating on some clearly defined strategic imperative?" But even at that, the model pioneered by the Apollo Groups of the for-profit world continues to dominate the marketplace. And, frankly, that model suggests that competition from for-profit providers will only get more intense.

With that as background, audience focus becomes the most critical place to start when developing a marketing plan. As we've explored in earlier chapters of this book, a branding initiative can be focused on very specific audiences and purposes, such as elevating the institutional profile for greater success in the student recruitment marketplace or enriching the perception of the institution among higher education leaders nationwide. These goals, established from the beginning of the marketing initiative, become the means to clearly define both how success will be measured and how resources will be allocated. Sometimes, when the initiative is very broad-scale and the resources aren't available to do all at once, the best way to start is with a "low fruit" approach: determining which targets are likely to be more easily met, as a way of both generating positive results and creating enthusiasm for the relevance of the program.

The reason for taking a clear look at audience focus is simple: A full-page *Wall Street Journal* ad—"impactful" as it might be—won't move a high school sophomore one micron, and a screamingly funny viral video on YouTube won't generally impress provosts nationwide or generate an eight-figure commitment from your top donor. So your plan has to orient itself to a target audience and a desired response you're trying to create in that audience. Strategy, broadly, provides the framework: how your institution can and will position itself based on your research and brand platform. Your key messages—authenticated, validated, and internally endorsed—are ready to be deployed. Now it's time to develop an actionable, segmented, bottom-line-focused brand marketing plan. And with all such plans, it's good to keep in mind Willie Sutton's reported reason for robbing banks: "because that's where the money is." A plan that is ROI-based will not only generate greater resources—because those resources are then seen as "investment" rather than pure "cost"—but will also give you clear means by which you can measure your success. But just as interesting to marketers, because it speaks to tactics, is another Willie Sutton aphorism: "You can't rob a bank on charm and personality"[5]—which is why he carried a Tommy gun. The lesson here? Know and use the right tools for the job at hand.

No book can write a brand marketing plan for you. Your plan will be entirely driven by your circumstances, your goals, and your resource availability. But as you consider how to flesh out your own plan, it's good to have as broad a view as possible of your options. And in terms of tactics, it's also useful to think of "traditional" and "emerging" media as you begin to scan the marketing channels. Among traditional media, include:

- Earned media
- Print advertising
- Out-of-home advertising (billboards, mallscapes, bus boards, etc.)
- Broadcast advertising (radio and television)
- Institutional print publications
- Direct marketing
- Web presence
- Events and event promotion

Among emerging media—a list that's bound to be out of date between the time I clatter these keys and this book is published—count:

- Online display ads and keyword search
- Podcasts
- Blogs and vlogs
- YouTube and other video file-sharing options
- MySpace, Facebook, and other social networking sites
- Instant messaging (IM)
- Twitter and other social networking/microblogging utilities
- Texting/SMS (Short Message Service) options
- Word-of-mouth marketing (as a deliberate discipline)
- Viral and guerrilla channels
- Something new that's only being invented *right now*!

Rather than tackling these one by one, let's look at them in the context of audience.

ACADEMICS, INFLUENCERS, AND *MACHERS*

Academics, influencers, and *machers* (a wonderful Yiddish term that means, essentially, a "big shot," often self-appointed) tend to be older, more fixed in their media habits, and, perhaps, more set in their opinions than their 16-year-old kids or grandkids. Demographically, they parallel the population at large, with an emphasis on Boomer and early-X generations—though because of embedded societal issues they tend to be more white, more male, and more well-compensated than the average American in the same age cohort.

Academics generally have an earned sense of accomplishment, a professional or disciplinary focus, and a career history through which they evaluate the achievements of others. For a quick group photo, take a look at the senior administrators, deans, and department chairs at your own institution. In all likelihood, they look much like the senior administrators, deans, and department chairs at competing and aspirant institutions. Their touch points are generally very traditional and require heavy lifting by your public affairs staff and at the departmental level—the latter in terms of enabling academic leaders to successfully campaign for research presentations and panel discussions at conferences.

- Earned print media, particularly the *Chronicle of Higher Education*, *New York Times*, *Washington Post*, *Wall Street Journal*, and major regional dailies such as the *Chicago Tribune*, *Los Angeles Times*, *Dallas Morning News* and others with a broad circulation base are still effective with these audiences—particularly those outlets that can also be retrieved online.

- "Expert" appearances on broadcast media add gravitas, including CNN, PBS, NPR (especially *Morning Edition*, *All Things Considered*, and *Marketplace*); news and information programming on NBC, CBS, ABC, and Fox, at the national and affiliate level; and national radio syndication networks.

- Presence in peer journals and on the podium at national and regional conferences organized around their specific discipline is most important within the disciplines.

- Advertising outreach to this group is very expensive, since there are few targeted means to reach them—and even in the *Chronicle* you're buying a lot of eyeballs further down the food chain.

- Web presence is essential to reaching this group, who are very savvy about the Web and use it as part of their scholarly and research process. The visual or design elements of your Web site should reflect a certain stature. It's not just that overuse of Flash or other animation techniques is a bit tacky; it will also frustrate the ability to get to the information itself, since animation isn't read by Web crawlers, and search engine optimization is critical to building a robust Web presence.

- Direct marketing—usually in the form of sending annual or president's reports directly to senior administrators at other institutions—is pretty pricey and generally not highly effective. If you want to see why, go in to your own president's office and 1) ask to see the major glossy reports received in the office during the past six months; then, 2) ask how many of them he or she has read. In our experience, the answers are, respectively, "about 18 inches of them" and "next to none."

- Events and event promotion can hold real benefit with this market segment, particularly in the form of institutionally hosted symposia or colloquia about relevant topics in higher ed administration, research disciplines, or cross-disciplinary initiatives. To promote such events, advertising, keyword search, and direct marketing all can have significant benefit, and getting other academic leaders to campus can pay huge and long-lasting rewards in terms of awareness, perception, and value.

Influencer as a category covers a wide range of individuals: from guidance counselors, teachers, and parents (for student recruitment purposes); to corporate leaders, recruiters, and civic partners (for career services and town/gown goals); to corporate R&D heads (for research contracts); to elected and agency officials (for legislative matters and government-sponsored research); to key media representatives. Influencers in many ways resemble academics in their media appetites, though they are less likely to focus on higher education media or disciplinary conferences, and local luminaries are more likely to also be influenced by mentions in local and regional papers and magazines and on local broadcast outlets. Guidance counselors are generally very in touch with students, and they know what type of students have succeeded and been happy at your institution and what type haven't. They tend to encourage the "professional" approach to distributing applications: two or three "stretch" schools, two or three "likely" schools, and two or three "safety" schools. They incessantly search the media—rankings, Peterson's, Fiske, Pope—and tour Web sites. Parents want their kids to be happy and to make a selection the family can afford. They will be led by their children's inquiry process (though they might have to step in and organize it). Corporate leaders, recruiters, and civic partners will be influenced by earned media in reputable publications, and R&D heads and agency representatives will pay attention to peer-reviewed journals. For many of these groups, paid media also start to play a role in creating an impression, reinforcing a brand, and softening the market for subsequent direct approaches.

- Print advertising, properly targeted, can deliver a solid brand impression. In fact, advertising of all types is one of the most effective ways to control your brand presentation. Unlike earned media, an ad will have in it only those elements you put there, not an interpretation delivered through the filter of a reporter or media representation. If only it wasn't so darned expensive ...

  To have an impact on local civic and business leaders, regional *Wall Street Journal* buys or display ads in a local business weekly or monthly can position the institution as a "player"—but make sure your creative team knows that the goal is to increase understanding of the civic role and economic impact of your institution, not to generate new applications. In the broadcast media, NPR underwriting provides a reasonable means to get through to influencers, particularly if you can sponsor the local broadcast of *Marketplace or Morning Edition* or any of the other news (rather than culture) segments—though the NPR audience skews both affluent and liberal. To get to the affluent and conservative segment, local "news talk" radio might be an alternative, though the cost is often significantly higher.

- Out-of-home advertising—particularly billboards on well-traveled highways or display ads in airports—can both capture attention and signal brand positioning. These are "snapshot" media, however. Blasting along in the passing lane at 70 mph or dashing through the terminal on the way to a meeting are not activities that allow for nuanced consideration or extended contemplation. Your brand platform has to be thoroughly distilled (see chapter 7, "Brand Activation") in order for it to be effective in these "drive-by" media.

The category of *machers* includes trustees and regents, advisory board members, donors and prospects, as well as some civic leaders and elected officials. Many of the tactics addressed above—earned media, events, print and out-of-home advertising—are also effective for this group, but those efforts can be buttressed by another classic technique: institutional print publications.

- Annual reports, president's reports, and "sexy" strategic plans can act as very effective orientation materials for *machers*, many of whom are only marginally or occasionally focused on the mission, activities, and accomplishments of the institution. Used as mailed outreach or leave-behinds after conversations with institutional leadership, they are more likely to be flipped through than thoroughly read, and they'll either find a place on the *macher's* coffee table or in a lobby materials rack (if there is pride in the association) or they'll soon be in the trash or recycle bin.

- Web presence is important to all audience segments now, and sophisticated SEO, intuitive architecture, strong brand messaging, and captivating graphics are necessary. For SEO, we now emphasize that Web sites need to be "slippery"—that is, they must offer plentiful opportunities to be picked up by aggregating Web sites through RSS feeds, linked blogs, metatags, and other methods. Flash and other animation can enliven a site, but too much Flash or too many extended, nonskippable intros can exhaust the patience of the searcher—particularly if these elements show up every time you return to the home page. With Web presence as with any other medium, you must start with this question: What message do we want this site to send, and with what audience are we trying to connect? Admittedly, with the Web, the answer to this question can be complicated. How do we develop a site that meets the needs of deans, donors, and D&D-minded teens? Many institutions have solved this conundrum by differentiating the "formal" Web site from the student recruitment site and having the Flash, bells and whistles, and interactive community function on the recruitment site—at an entirely different URL—rather than on the main site. Such segmentation, supported by direct marketing and other support that drives the target audience to the appropriate site, can have links that allow searchers to move readily into the more formal presentation of the university after they've had their whistle wetted on the parallel "consumer" site.

In the end, with *machers*, you want direct involvement: one-on-one or small group conversations, receptions at the home of a major supporter or in some "privileged" setting (such as an after-hours gathering at a blockbuster art exhibition or seats in the president's box for the homecoming game), tours that feature both administrative leaders and faculty members who can lead lively lectures about the antiquities or cultures observed through the porthole, or other opportunities to get your top people in close conversation with them. Listening to their interests and concerns is essential, and responding appropriately—through what is known in the fundraising world as "moves management"—will drive the engagement to the next level.

Brand as the User Experience

As we navigate the Internet's teen years, it's worth noting that executing *brand* on the Web has proven tough for everyone. The commercial world is littered with colossal failures—enough to prompt several annual "Worst of" lists, as well as a significant slew of blog entries and studies.

Why is it so hard? Because it's complex. Brand expression online is a matter of *the user experience*—the cumulative experience a visitor has as he or she tries to learn something, find something, or do something on your Web site. It's not a matter of having four Flash modules on the admissions page or professors who Twitter (although these might be good ideas). It's a matter of the visitor's full experience on your site and whether that experience meets expectations that are organic to your brand.

With that definition in hand, what kind of online experience do we expect of Accenture, celebrated as one of the top 50 global commercial brands and a master of technology? Naturally, Accenture's smart, systems-savvy brand suggests that we'll experience firsthand the company's command of technology and sophisticated understanding of the world. We expect an interaction that is well-thought-out and nearly seamless; we want to navigate easily, scan the full scope of research instantly, and use a smart, customized tool to sort through the complex content efficiently.

None of this happens. Instead (at the time of this writing) we fumble through inaccessible and outdated fly-out navigation, we have to search hard for Accenture's recent successes, and we struggle to get past the barrier of the tone-deaf home page, which showcases the company's sponsorship of the World Golf Championship during a global recession.

As a user experience, Accenture.com belies the company's slogan: "High performance. Delivered." It's not high performance, nor is there much in the way of delivery.

For colleges and universities, this insight— the brand as user experience—can cut two ways. Certainly, it's a challenge. It suggests greater investment in online channels than has been typical in the last decade. It requires a concerted institutional effort to understand the brand as an active and interactive presence; it demands coordination among offices that manage online channels and a disciplined program of measurement and adjustment. Responsibility for the institutional Web site must rest with the marketing and communications group working with collaborative Web developers who understand the user experience. It's a tall order.

But understanding brand as the user experience can also be freeing. It invites institutions to cook up true brand expressions rather than chase the latest fad. (For a true and original brand expression, take a look at Trinity University's Thinkmap, an innovative use of mapping that enables the visitor to experience the campus' close-knit community rather than wade through indistinguishable student profiles.) Brand as user experience also helps institutions avoid the hazard of focusing on departments rather than the people they serve—prospective students and their parents, alumni, faculty and staff, students, and community. And focusing on people can be only be good for the institution overall.

Lee Reilly
Vice President, Interactive
Lipman Hearne

FACULTY, STAFF, AND CURRENT STUDENTS

Your internal audiences—faculty, staff, and current students—can make or break a branding campaign. Involving them early, as both informants and reviewers, can help guarantee the *authenticity* of the brand. Keeping them involved, through presentations and discussions, by contributing to the build-out of the attributes highlighted in the brand platform, by sharing appropriate research with them and encouraging them to talk with their colleagues so they get comfortable with the brand messaging, will help make them brand ambassadors rather than brand busters.

But these groups are leery of being "marketed to." They believe that they have a more acute understanding of the institution than any outsider could possibly have; and while they are generally right in this view, they are also not likely to understand or accept the potential bias in their own perspective. Faculty members, in particular, occupy a privileged position. If tenured, they are immune from the marketplace and tend to focus on the relatively insular world of their own discipline. That obsession with the minutiae of their own scholarship is what makes them great, but it also makes the "in-selling" process much more laborious and incremental than it might otherwise be.

The key to any such in-selling is the authenticity of the brand platform—and the validation you can muster in terms of a wide variety of programs and features that are consistent with that brand platform. And don't forget self-interest. In my experience, once internal audiences realize the many benefits of a strengthened or sharpened brand, they are ready and willing to get on board, though they of course come armed with their perspectives and ready-made solutions that are not necessarily cognizant of market perceptions or realities.

One of the best ways to start the discussion and trigger acceptance among these groups is through an intensive, well-timed brand workshop. The critical elements to making such a workshop effective include these:

- **Launch from the top.** The brand must have the endorsement and backing of the president, chancellor, or CEO, and his or her voice must be the first one heard at the brand workshop.

- **Review of goals.** Present an overview of the specific goals that the branding initiative was formed to address.

- **Review of relevant research.** Highlights of the research—including both methodology (segmentation, sample size, etc.) and relevant findings—are widely seen as objective and unimpeachable and can go a long way toward creating a shared, market-based understanding of the current positioning of the brand.

- **Presentation or discussion of brand platform.** A built-out brand platform, with its presentation of icons and attributes, features and benefits, acts as a useful mnemonic device for capturing the salient elements of the brand.

- **Small group breakouts.** Divide the gathering into breakout groups to deal with specific aspects of the brand platform—such as developing the expressions and metrics as they relate to brand attributes—and then have them report to the entire gathering. The approach provides a mechanism by which subsets (by department, function, etc.) can drill down into the brand platform and discover how it applies to them. The process of investigation and reporting also helps build understanding and buy-in.

You can also bring your internal audiences into alignment with the brand through an orchestrated "brand launch" process, an editorial board with the student newspaper, and campus banners and tchotchkes if and when the creative expression (see next chapter) is ready. The keys here are recognition ("this really fits me") and celebration ("I like me!"). Remember, the brand needs to be positioned as the hero in the individual's narrative—the agency through which each participant or stakeholder achieves that singular dream.

PROSPECTIVE STUDENTS

Now we get into what is the real nitty-gritty for many colleges and universities. For independent schools, parents play a critical role in the decision-making process, but our research indicates that while the current generation of students will often speak of "our" family decision in regard to their college choice, the parents are actually facilitators of the decision, rather than actually participants in making it.

So the job, as always, is getting the prospect to campus. All the research shows that this is where the deal is closed—on the walkway, under the elms (or oaks or magnolias), as that hottie/hunk walks by and the tour guide ("Puh-leeze! No walking backward!") delivers the spiel. Remember, it's experiential, and you're asking the young people walking in the group to believe that their future is fullest on your campus, with your faculty, with these peers.

But how to get them to campus? Constant contact, continuing engagement and community transactions, always asking. In terms of specific media channels:

- Earned media: Not.
- Print advertising: So "my grandma"—unless it's in a source that seems close at hand, such as the high school or community college newspaper.
- Out-of-home advertising: Mallscapes, bus boards, banners—yeah! As long as it's cool and the kids are hot.
- Broadcast advertising: So, do you sound like the announcer on KISS-FM?
- Institutional print publications: Not as important at the search stage, but crucial to yield—and yo, dude, the viewbook's a mirror, not a window.
- Direct marketing: Is it cool? Can I get it quick? Is it funny – har-har, not eee-uww? Can I thumbtack it to my bulletin board?
- Web presence: Absolutamente.
- Online display ads and keyword search: If you're not doing that, you must not care about me.

- Podcasts: Borrrrring. Unless it's Fall Out Boy playing your alma mater.
- Blogs and vlogs: UGC? Yeah, hombre. But that "approved" institutional junk? Fuggedaboutit!
- Facebook and Youtube: That's my space—what are you doing in it? And don't you dare look at those photos of me partying with my buds ... that's not for your snoopy eyes!
- IM: How'd you get my number? Creep!
- Texting and Twitter: Ditto.
- Word-of-mouth marketing: Whatchoo talkin' 'bout?
- Videogame inserts: Yeow! I can blow up your billboard? Awesome!

The social media space is evolving faster than can be captured in a book. Today's teens live in a constant barrage of media, simultaneously texting, IMing, talking on the phone, manipulating their iTunes playlists, watching YouTube, and driving their parents crazy (I speak from experience). For this traditional age student—particularly those who reside at the desirable demographic crossroads of "ready to succeed" and "able to pay"—ADHD is the new Franklin Covey and any diversion is welcome, as long as it doesn't plan to stick around too long. My teenage daughter has gone from preferring Harvard (it's the best, after all), to Oregon State (it's just over the hill from my cousin's horse ranch), to Columbia ("If you can make it there ..."), to who knows where by the time this book is published or it reaches your hands. She, like many, is searching—for herself, not for you—and she won't know what she wants until she finds it, tries it on, and likes herself in the mirror. Your job: be in sight, maybe only on the periphery, consistently, until she's ready to pay real attention. Then make sure you have the answer to her questions. In this regard, a social media presence is important as "backgrounding" to a more traditional, in-depth search and selection process. Research shows that only 18 percent of students use social media in their college search process[6] and that Facebook and similar pages rank 28th out of 30 information sources in that influence yield—but six of the top 10 influential sources are driven by word-of-mouth.[7] The inference here is that the more dimensional portrait that you create through print materials, direct conversations on campus and at college fairs, Web presence, and other institutional touch points is what really drives the decision—but that being active in a social media context can help you be part of the conversation.

For the nontraditional student, the more traditional avenues still work, with the addition of online advertising, paid search terms, and sophisticated SEO. Print advertising, job fairs, direct mail: all still work with this important, career-oriented demographic.

With prospective students of all types—as well as with all groups for whom you have complex, multidimensional marketing initiatives—the key is intelligent and effective *tactical sequencing*. You must always make sure you have a specific desired outcome from each target and tactical element so that the call to action is clear and your institution can measure how many members of the target audience take the desired action—whether that's going to a Web site, requesting more information, coming to an open house, touring campus, applying for special scholarships or more generalized financial aid, or applying and subsequently enrolling. This specificity will help you determine the anticipated ROI of your tactical mix and will allow you to make the case for ongoing marketing investments even in tough economic times by providing you with the kind of "cash on the barrelhead" results that are triggered by your marketing efforts.

All too often, organizations continue to make the marketing investments they've typically made—whether it's attendance at college fairs, production of a wide variety of print materials, advertising in college guides, or any of a myriad of other recruitment communications options—without being able to measure the effect of their activities. So when bad budget times roll around, the marketing or recruitment officers are hard-pressed to justify their spending because they can't point directly to the revenue impact of their strategies and tactics. They can't answer the question "What would we lose if we reduced your budget 10 percent?" And, if asked to reduce the budget 10 percent, they wouldn't have a scientific or market-based rationale for making the necessary cuts. Descartes reasoned that a thrown spear would never pierce its target if the distance between them was cut in half, then cut in half again, then again *ad infinitum*. There would always be a micron that could be further divided in half before the point would actually penetrate the fabric. Descartes wasn't talking about budgets, though: Each subsequent slash—halfway or not—causes major repercussions, and eventually the chief marketing officer will take that spear in the chest.

ALUMNI

Alumni relations are the subject of many books already, a great majority of them available from CASE. And as any alumni officer worth her Blahniks would tell you, good alumni relations begin with the on-campus experience—in the classroom and out—and the visibility or importance that's attached to alumni engagement during the student's time on campus.

Listen and Learn

No amount of great messaging or communications can make up for really bad memories. Example: For one public university client, who had experienced significant campus turmoil in the Vietnam War era and whose administration had actively been involved in a fairly brutal response to campus protests, our research led us to tell them, "Never contact those people again." Thirty years later, they were still bitter, still mad, and still saying bad things about the place. Better you should forget them. Those folks who want to find their way back will do so. For the others, you're wasting your stamps and just roiling the waters.

Taken as a whole, the alumni communications enterprise is best considered as part of a broader customer relationship management strategy on the part of the alumni relations and development offices. And in that discussion of alumni CRM strategies come into play the many things **we w**ant from alumni: an enthusiastic regard for the institution, a willingness to involve themselves in institutional initiatives, a fierce protectionism when the institution is threatened, a readiness to volunteer in recruitment or advancement activities, a yearning to send their own kids to their alma mater, and oh yes—an invariably positive response when asked to contribute to the annual fund or capital initiatives.

We don't want much from them, do we?

And what do we offer in return? Sometimes, a lot: an active involvement in the life of the institution, access to new thinking and dynamic faculty, energy and enthusiasm from involvement with students, an exciting vision for the institution as expressed by its key leaders, inordinate pride in wearing the institutional "badge" on their c.v. and spirit wear. Sometimes, not much: an annual solicitation mailing and nothing else—unless you're a dues-paying member of the alumni association.

Research conducted by Lipman Hearne in 2007 among more than 1,000 alumni of institutions throughout the country, all of whom hold advanced degrees, offers some key insights into the reasons why alumni give or don't give to the institution from which they earned their degrees. As table 1 shows, alumni pride and appreciation are the highest-ranking drivers of alumni giving to both public and private institutions, though agreement in rationale for publics and privates begins to differ as you slide down the scale. Significantly, donors to private institutions are far more likely to consider financial aid to students a strong motivator to giving, especially when they received such aid themselves, while donors to public institutions are more likely to regard payback for a good career as a driver. An oft-cited rationale—"maintaining the value of your degree"—rates very low among givers, as does the tax benefit of making a gift.

When level of giving is considered, the importance of targeted messaging becomes even more apparent, as table 2 shows. For larger annual gifts, strong motivators include alumni pride, to show appreciation, ensure quality education, importance of the institution, payback, and financial need, as well as the tax benefit of the gift.

Finally, when giving behaviors are correlated with attitude toward the institution, a strong argument emerges for an engaged and effective alumni communications program. Among all donors, and felt particularly strongly by those who give $500 per year or more, pride, connectivity ("keeps me informed," "strong connection," "part of community"), and interest are closely linked with donative behavior (see table 3). And among those who don't give, "only hear from them when asking for money" is a persistent complaint.

Table 1. Reasons for Giving to Alma Mater

	Public (N=158)	Private (N=161)
Proud to be an alum	**69%**	**76%**
To show appreciation	69%	71%
Asked to contribute	51%	57%
Institution plays an important role	50%	54%
Ensure quality education for future students	43%	60%
Response to solicitation	38%	40%
Alumni donations are used for financial aid	26%	**42%**
Payback for a good career	**38%**	25%
For tax benefit	27%	22%
Financial needs of institution compelling	18%	22%
Received financial aid	9%	17%
Maintain/improve value of degree	14%	12%

Table 2. Motivators for Giving

	Donation to Undergrad Institute		
	Under $100 (N=104)	$100-$499 (N=126)	$500+ (N=80)
To show appreciation	66%	72%	66%
Proud to be an alum	66%	67%	**88%**
Response to solicitation	57%	39%	19%
Asked to contribute	53%	65%	37%
Ensure quality education for future students	47%	54%	54%
Institution plays an important role	36%	51%	**58%**
Alumni donations used for financial aid	32%	36%	35%
Payback for a good career	21%	29%	**46%**
Received financial aid	17%	9%	16%
Financial needs of institution compelling	14%	14%	**36%**
Maintain/improve value of degree	13%	8%	17%
For tax benefit	12%	29%	**42%**

Table 3. Attitudes Toward Alma Mater

	Donation to Undergrad Institute		
	None	$1-$499	$500+
	(N=104)	(N=126)	(N=80)
Proud to be an alum	71%	**92%**	**95%**
Grateful for opportunities	70%	90%	95%
Experience contributed to success today	67%	88%	**93%**
Only hear from them when asking for money	**52%**	33%	34%
Strong interest in future success	49%	**84%**	**89%**
Keeps me informed	49%	**86%**	87%
Merits strong support	45%	**87%**	**91%**
Strong connection to institution	43%	**80%**	88%
Very interested in what's going on	38%	**80%**	**91%**
Makes me feel like part of community	31%	**64%**	**73%**
Personal responsibility to keep institution great	28%	**76%**	**89%**

This is not to say that directing more dollars to flow into the annual fund should be the end-all, be-all of alumni communications, but it does mean that giving—as a clear and simple indicator of brand affiliation—can be greatly affected by your marketing effort. Clear messages, frequent points of contact (especially those that are not asking for a gift), and an invitation to continue to be part of the large alma mater community will go a long way toward generating the kind of relationship that will result in active, engaged, and generous alumni. As one fundraiser friend of mine says, "Gifts are the profit of the relationship"—and a brand communications program that reminds alumni of the enduring values and impact of the institution will only enhance that relationship.

And for all audiences, an authentic brand positioning, delivered through compelling creative that's deployed across all brand touch points, will only improve the institutional profile.

---

1. A.C. Nielsen, Top 10 Advertisers—by U.S. Spending on Tradition Media, from "The Nielsen Company Issues Top Ten U.S. Lists for 2007," press release, Dec. 11, 2007.

2. Apollo Group, *Annual Report 2007*, 60.

3. Ibid., 30.

4. Lipman Hearne/CASE Marketing Survey, *Key Insights*, April 2007.

5. Willie Sutton with Edward Linn, *Where the Money Was: The Memoirs of a Bank Robber* (New York: Viking Press, 1976), 130.

6. College Board/Art & Science Group, student poll, January 2009.

7. Lipman Hearne, *High-Achieving Seniors and the College Decision*, October 2009.

CHAPTER 7

BRAND ACTIVATION

OK. YOU UNDERSTAND HOW YOUR BRAND IS POSITIONED relative to that of your competitors. You've figured out functional attributes and emotional drivers. You've distilled the brand reward and sketched the brand personality. Now, how do you bring the brand to life?

In a word? *Magic!*

Not really—though often the transition from the analytics and logic of branding to the creative expression of the brand has an underlying hint of abracadabra. In this chapter, we'll try to take apart that magic without leaving it in sundered (and sundried), meaningless chunks strewn around the office table—much like a skillful literary critic would disassemble a Shakespearean sonnet and show how it works while still letting it resonate with all its *a-b-a-b* sonority.

CREATIVE BRIEF

Brand activation begins with brand expression, and brand expression begins with the creative brief. Built off the brand platform, the creative brief provides guidelines that members of the creative team can follow as they begin to "animate" the brand. A good creative brief is written by someone (or someones) intimately familiar with institutional goals, market research, functional attributes, and emotional drivers of the brand. Often, in the best of circumstances, the creative brief is a collaborative effort between the account director—that person who has shepherded the branding initiative through all stages since its inception—and a creative director who has had the opportunity to "ride along" on many of the key goal-setting, research, and platform development steps. This combination is powerful because it brings together the deep, syncretic insights of both the left and the right hemispheres of the "branding brain" and provides a thorough, dimensional portrait of what the brand has to be able to do as it engages the market.

The creative brief should provide the answers to five key questions:

1. What do we want the communication to *do*? What is the institutional goal for this brand expression? (i.e., engage the interest of prospective students, cause nondonor alumni to contribute to the annual fund, cause donor alumni to increase their gift commitment, etc.)

2. To whom are we talking? What insights do we have about them?

3. How do we want the brand to come across? How do we want the target audience to talk about its functional and emotional benefits? How do we want the target audience to describe the reward of association with the brand?

4. What's the single most important thing we want the target audience to take away from the communication, and how can we make this believable?

5. In what medium or media will the communication be executed? What are the timeline and budget requirements that must be considered in the creative process?

Any creative director worth his or her Salty Dog would welcome a creative brief that fully fleshes out answers to these questions, as well as to a catchall query: Is there anything else worth thinking about that might help us do great and exciting work?

Then comes the fun part.

BRAINSTORMING

There are all kinds of fancy ways to describe this generative process. Ideation. Creative improvisation. Applied imagination. But whatever you call it, the elements are the same:

- A group of people
- A problem
- A room with a big whiteboard or multiple sheets of sticky-back paper
- A lot of M&M's—though some prefer Skittles

The process isn't random, however. A good brainstorm session is as carefully organized as a brand presentation, and generally more fun. It starts with determining who is most crucial to the effort—the account director and the creative director, obviously, but after that it's a combination of left- and right-brain assets. Somebody from the research area—particularly the focus group moderator or somebody else who was deeply immersed in the qualitative intake. Somebody who represents the media through which the brand will be transmitted. People with varying creative skill sets—a designer and/or interactive strategist and/or copy-writer. Somebody fun. Somebody serious. Somebody with extra Skittles. And somebody who's in charge: you.

Brainstorming and Creative Generation

Your presence has been requested at a brainstorming session—or some kind of meeting where the goal is idea generation. Will it yield brilliance, perhaps even bring about a paradigm shift? Or will it be, in the words of a video store clerk describing *Eyes Wide Shut*, "two hours of your life you'll never get back"?

Below are some brainstorming guideposts I've found helpful. Note that missing from this list is one that everyone has heard before: "No idea is too silly." Actually, I think you can lose a lot of time and momentum on silly, generic ideas. If you start out with some ground rules, you avoid burnout after the first 45 minutes.

Think mantra, not manufacturing process.
Nike tells us "Just do it"—not how to do it or what materials constitute their shoes.

Spend some time in the big room.
Everyone should bring inspiration from the outside world into the brainstorming room. I find the materials most useful when they are *not* from an organization's orbit. The corporate world drops millions of dollars on message, branding, and trend research, and shapes the way we take in all messages. Attention must be paid.

Use what you own.
No one else has your name (I hope). One of your brainstorming "buckets" should be built around your name, whether it's through alliteration or making a word in your name come to life in a new way. It may sound trite, but your audiences have a lot to remember these days. You can make it easy for them—and build your brand at the same time.

Ask your audience to create meaning.
Wordplay tickles our intellect, but a truly great idea opens up a dialogue with the audience. Most taglines, for example, are like old sitcoms: They tell the audience when to laugh. But the TV shows that have dominated the popular imagination lately—*Lost*, *The Sopranos*—invite the audience to become part of the story. Don't nail down your idea so solidly that the audience can't engage in the give-and-take of a conversation. Think about how your idea can resonate in intriguing ways, cajoling and empowering a message-weary audience to answer the Big Question—What's in it for me?—on their own terms.

Be assumptive and assertive.
This ground rule is not a contradiction of the point above. Essentially, we're asking audiences to hang out with an idea—and who wants to hang with a milquetoast? As the great philosopher Mel Brooks said, "If you walk up to the bell, you gotta ring it."

Only one idea can walk through the door at a time.
And that doorway is getting ever narrower, as audiences seek to thwart entry by the barrage of messages. There are many, many important things you want to say to your audience. But what's the one thing you need to say first, to get you past the threshold? To use another metaphor, if your idea has to pay too many pipers, a brain-storm isn't going to fix things; your strategy needs an overhaul.

No one has ever complained "Not another way to eat chocolate!"
A lot of nonprofits share the same qualities—attentiveness, responsiveness, a commitment to making life better. These are all good qualities. Think of them as chocolate. Now, what's a new way to experience chocolate?

Offer membership in a club.
Affiliation beats description in terms of emotional resonance. Forget what Groucho Marx said. Everyone wants to belong to something. How can your idea help people self-identify?

Own a cultural truth.
Reality shows capture people's imagination, not just because they flatter our desires for voyeurism and schadenfreude, but also because they expose and reaffirm enduring truths. Look for ideas and attitudes that are in common currency and give them new meaning. One of my all-time favorite taglines belongs to the Peace Corps: "The Toughest Job You'll Ever Love."

...which is different from telling audiences something they already know.
When I worked on the Liquid-Plumr account, we wasted a lot of energy coming up with words that tried to convince people that hair clogs are bad. Of course people know hair clogs are bad! What are you going to do about it? The solution: a campaign called "The plumber to call first." (And it showcases the product name, too.)

Libby Morse
Senior Creative Director
Lipman Hearne

Good brainstorm sessions are time-limited. This creates a sense of purpose and defined outcome that a meandering meeting can't. Sixty minutes works best, though you don't need a ticking clock and Andy Rooney to enforce the deadline. Urgency creates intensity. The creative brief would have been distributed in advance—and supplied again for those who "forgot" to bring them—as would the agenda. And the agenda is not open-ended. It doesn't have as a goal "some great ideas for an influencer billboard or maybe a new prospective student microsite." The goal must be specific: "three ideas for execution as print ads in the next 30 days"; "three concepts for a halftime spot airing November 7"; "three viewbook concepts for testing on April 15."

The brainstorm starts on time. You lay out the rules.

- Our goal is xxxx.
- We have 60 minutes.
- We're not looking for perfection; we're looking for idea generation.
- All ideas are good ideas—even the really bad ones. (Some of the best ideas come out of jokes or riffing on "warts" of the institution—which are distinctive and can be seen, in another light, as true beauty marks.)
- No arguments over the relative merit of ideas.
- Ideas are free-range—they are no one's property.
- The Skittles are fair game.

Your role as facilitator in the first 30 minutes is to keep things moving, keep the idea generator chugging to produce a continuing current of creative electricity. Some tricks:

- "We've got that, let's move on."
- "We're getting hung up in a whole set of related ideas around xxxx. What else do we use as a jumping-off point?"
- "Does that come in red?"

- "We'll worry about execution later."
- "Put down the knife. Now!"
- "What are we missing?"
- "Let's look at the creative brief again. One minute of silence."
- "Does anyone want to see me toss a Skittle up in the air and catch it in my mouth?"

Of course, your ideas are also welcome. You're not just a scribe, you're also a contributor. Make sure, though, that you or your ideas don't dominate. You are not the expert or final voice but the accelerant, the gas in that idea generator.

The next 20 minutes are for clustering and cleaning. What are the groups of ideas that seem to revolve around one central concept? What are the weird, worthy outliers? What can be eliminated as redundant, irrelevant, dull, or "done that"? Which ideas really persist, tug at the group, or continue to kindle the imagination? Which just won't let go of you? (Note: In this process, more new ideas will also be generated. If they are good and new and fresh, get them on the board; if they are revisions of existing ideas, get the new version into the appropriate cluster.)

The goal of this clustering and cleaning process is to reduce the board from 20 or 30 or 60 scattershot ideas into a more controllable, more assessable set of six or eight that have continuing merit. To select among a handful of related ideas the one best representative of that set—the one that expresses it most effectively. To "clear the board" of distractions and blind alleys so that the last 10 minutes—when decisions are made about what ideas will go forward—is manageable. To identify the ideas that seem to have real life, distinction, and potential. (Often, the creative brief can come back into play as a filter in this process: Are there any issues in the timing or execution or medium that might eliminate some ideas—at least for now? Do ideas have to be shifted in some way to address these issues?)

Then, the final 10 minutes. Revisit the goal. Revisit the "deliverable" parameters in terms of deadline, medium, process or production issues. Are there some great ideas that simply don't fit the purpose? If yes, then put them in a "parking lot" for re-examination at another time. Do some ideas work much better than others in the planned medium? Are there ideas that are clearly keepers—ones that the whole group recognizes as having breakthrough potential? Is there one that stands so far above the rest that it's "game over"? Which are the two or three—or the number specified in your agenda—that are going to go forward into concept development?

Sometimes the finalists rise by acclaim and sometimes there's more muddle. Your job as facilitator is to help the group resolve that muddle and send forward the appropriate set of ideas for further development—and to thank people and send them back to the rest of their workday with the remaining Skittles.

What we're after in this regard is the meme—the core idea that's capable of replicating itself, of going viral, of having a life beyond the whiteboard, of generating great creative. Because that's what comes next.

CONCEPT DEVELOPMENT

Coming out of the brainstorm session, each selected meme should again be passed by the creative brief to ensure that the creative director in charge of developing that particular concept—assuming that you have a choice of creative directors—knows the where and what of the eventual application. And then a new formula comes into play: time x talent. While some ideas spring forth fully fleshed like Athena bursting from Zeus' forehead, others require more careful construction.

Generally, we try to move through concept development in three phases, which can perhaps best be seen in action. Let's say that one of the memes that came out of the brainstorm session was based around alumni sophistication and impact; let's call it "At Home in the World." One way to proceed is to develop that idea—alone or with a small team—by "spoking" the various directions that the idea could take.

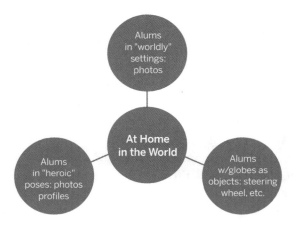

Sometimes, this is drawn like the diagram above, only with more spokes: alums in a group of people (students, employees, special needs individuals, etc.) on whom your alums have had an impact, an illustration of the globe with your university or college as "home," alums in the costume of their adopted lands (Mombasa, Mumbai, Madrid, Modesto). Sometimes it's just a series of notes with bullet points next to them. And at some point, certain of these spokes start to exert a gravitational pull, calling out, "Can't you just see me?"

And you know, you've just gotta start somewhere and hope for the snap, crackle, and pop of genius.

All the ideas must be developed in equivalent formats so that the format differences don't skew the testing process. Be careful of unintended consequences of imagery. For one client, validation testing was going astray because the photos in one execution suggested that the experience and the focus were primarily international. When we substituted those photos with a more "blended" mix, we got a very different result. In other words, compare ads to ads, viewbooks to viewbooks, billboards to billboards—and rest assured that your results will not send you down a pathway that you don't want to follow.

One thing to note: In these days of composition and layout by computer, it's easy to get beguiled into cooking ideas too far in this stage of the process. At this point, it's not about sublime execution, but about expression of concept. Because what you've got to do next— after you find the right photo or illustration, written the headline, chopped in some body copy, and mocked up the art or developed the storyboards—is testing. Because it's not about what you like or what your board thinks is right, unless they're the intended focus of the creative; it's about what generates the desired impression among those people whose perception you want to change or whose action you want to stimulate: your target audience. Whatever research method you use, you're seeking to find which concept has the greatest resonance, hits the audience most squarely, is most likely to engender the desired response.

That's your winner. That's the campaign you'll take to market—after, of course, extensive "proving up" of the idea, development of real copy, photo shoots or recording sessions, creative refinement, production and postproduction review and improvement.

And then it's all about cross-platform execution. How does this work on the Web? As a banner ad? As a direct mail piece? As the frame for a publication? In Flash? Twittered? To stimulate a social network with user generated content?

ACTIVATION IN ACTION

In our work with the University of Chicago Booth School of Business, the challenge was to differentiate the school from its many fine competitors, draw attention in the marketplace for its executive MBA and MBA offerings, and build off the strong brand of the university itself—a place long known for accommodating relentless brainiacs. The solution? Reinforce the idea that the Booth School (as it was named after a $300 million gift in late 2008 from a successful graduate) provided its graduates—some would say "survivors"—with all the tools they need when it came time for their "moment of truth" in the marketplace. The decision was made to use a very assertive, direct address approach, led by strong headlines rather than images.[1]

At Calvin College, the challenge was to present this dynamic, Christian institution as a place to pursue a truly challenging intellectual quest within the context of a strong faith community. The answer grew out of the idea "We're not afraid to explore the shades of grey."

At Kettering University—founded as General Motors Institute—the challenge became how to represent the energy and character of a co-op-based engineering program. The answer: "geek chic." The campaign brought a standing ovation from faculty and staff and greatly increased applications and yield soon after it was launched.

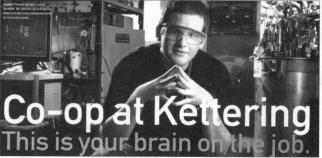

At Ball State University, market research revealed that the challenge was to position this mid-size public university in relation to two very distinct segments: the much larger public competitors at Indiana University, Indiana University–Purdue University Indianapolis, and Purdue University; and the smaller, private institutions that many students chose. The response? A tongue-in-cheek campaign focused on the Goldilocks answer: "Just right."

The success of this campaign was demonstrated in two ways. First, students responded, applied, and enrolled. Second, competitors picked up the phone and called Ball State to protest: "How dare you call us limited?" You know you're doing well when your competitors complain.

Successful campaigns such as these lead to related questions. How do you continue to refresh the idea? What are its extensions? How long do you maintain the campaign (usually far longer than your internal audience is comfortable with)?

And—the big one—how do you generate institutional will to launch and sustain a comprehensive branding campaign?

For that, see the next chapter.

---

1. For a closer look at these and other images in this book, as well as additional images related to the branding campaigns discussed in these chapters, go to *www.case.org* and enter CASE code "BrandImages."

CHAPTER 8

PUTTING IT ALL IN MOTION

ONE OF THE MOST DIFFICULT TASKS for any marketing manager in higher education is developing a budget to sustain an effective, broadly disseminated branding campaign. There are so many competing priorities. Faculty will argue that new faculty lines—or, better yet, across-the-board salary increases *and* new faculty lines—will do more for the institution than any outreach efforts. Students will wonder why the institution is spending so much to bring in more students who will compete with them for classes, attention, financial aid, and prime parking spaces. Alumni will want to know that the outreach is going to add value to their degree and enhance their bragging rights. Donors will want to know that their investments are going to raise the quality of a program rather than its visibility—unless that program carries their name. And leadership will be mindful that any marketing investment will have to be justified in the eyes of these observers—and more.

Forward-thinking marketing managers will engage with leaders from those administrative units most likely to benefit from an improved brand presence: enrollment management, alumni affairs, development, and external relations—as well as the president's office. Spend some time in "blue sky" conversations with them about the issues that keep them up at night—and how a stronger brand might address some of those issues. Make their problems your problems. Design a brand initiative that includes direct market research with their constituencies (or incorporates a deep dive into their existing research)—always remembering the dictum "What do we want to do with the data?" Build a plan with both "low fruit" immediacy and longer-term impact.

But most of all: track.

At the University of Cincinnati, one of the most powerful tools in supporting a successful branding campaign has been to keep careful track of ROI-based marketing investments and results. Mary Stagaman, associate vice president for community relations and marketing, focused on two primary goals for UC's branding initiative: increasing and diversifying regional perception of the university, and reversing historic downward trends in enrollment. Public perception research before the launch of the branding initiative established that many stellar programs—such as the schools of design, architecture, and planning; the colleges of medicine and allied health; the conservatory of music—were not closely associated in the public mind with the university. Attributes and programs that registered high in unaided recall were "big" and "basketball." On top of this, the university had been struggling for years to attract the best and brightest students from the metropolitan region and beyond.

Enter our branding champion. Stagaman's service to the university began in 1985, when she signed on as director of college relations at the Raymond Walters campus. With her move to the main campus, she was assigned to accelerate a branding initiative that was already in motion.

"Before I came on board, we had hired LPK—an international design agency founded by UC grads—to develop a new brand identity. Their insights on how a fully leveraged brand identity can have a very great effect on building a brand have been incredibly helpful—and they've given us tools from the beginning to provide some discipline to our identity program," said Stagaman in an interview.

With that identity system in place, the next stage was to build greater campus buy-in for a more coherent, branded communications stream that would present a new face to the market—one emphasizing discovery and transformation. The first step was to simply illustrate the problem. "We put together an 'envelope test' that demonstrated how our materials and communications displayed a complete cacophony of styles, colors, messages, and execution levels. There was no sense that the materials came from a single institution, and very few of the materials really represented the quality that we knew to be inherent here. And so many colleges and units had developed their own identity marks, we had come to a point I called 'logo soup,'" Stagaman recalled. The branding team also took advantage of a growing awareness on campus that the institution's reputation was not commensurate with its quality and that the brand was being dictated by competitors and by outdated perceptions, rather than by a focused, strategic institutional effort.

The message set that developed from the branding team's internal investigation and market research was straightforward:

The University of Cincinnati provides—

• Many pathways for success

• Real-world experience

• Intellectual exchange of ideas

• Quality education and research

Moreover, the University is singularly focused on improving the lives and expanding the options for people and institutions in Cincinnati and the region.

Early in the process, Stagaman and her colleagues reached out to staff members throughout the university who had the word *communications* in their job title or who were otherwise charged with expression and outreach. "If you think you're a communicator, you're welcome in our tent," became the philosophy. Stagaman's team developed and distributed tools online that made brand adherence very simple, and a series of workshops provided individuals from throughout the institution with the knowledge they needed to work with the new brand platform.

Another key was the associate deans, whom Stagaman calls the COOs of the colleges. "We worked really hard to get their buy-in," said Stagaman. Other workshops focused on how to live the brand through special events, how to write to the brand, how to make sure that photography was appropriate to the brand. After one workshop for media representatives, a grizzled, 30-year veteran of the *Cincinnati Enquirer* paid the effort a journalist's highest compliment: "This was not lame."

The fundamental strategy that the university pursued was to "change the story," shifting the portrayal of the institution from a solid, acceptable fallback school to a viable first-choice option for many highly qualified students. "We raised the bar and the students came with us," stated Stagaman. The university logged more than three years of record enrollments, both in terms of quantity and quality. A dynamic building program—which caused architectural critics to describe the campus as a "veritable outdoor museum of contemporary architecture"[1]— underscored the transformation theme, as did the relentless efforts of the university's best spokesperson: President Nancy L. Zimpher. According to Stagaman, "The president did 480 presentations in her first year in office. She's a spectacular storyteller. People in the city believe she wears black and red [UC's colors] every day. Her visibility has been a major tool and driver in reframing and reshaping our brand in people's minds."

A media campaign framed around the concept "It's All UC" established a new signature for innovation and quality programs for the university. A refocusing of public relations efforts both in terms of content (greater emphasis on transformative programs and teaching and research initiatives) and medium (more Web, less print) also helped shape the public image of the institution. And it worked. In research conducted in late 2008, "big" had been replaced by "good academic reputation" as the top attribute associated with the university in the minds of alumni, parents, and prospects.

The lessons from Stagaman's experience at the University of Cincinnati can be extended to virtually any institution.

- **Understand your strengths.** Research, accept, admit, and build on those attributes or understandings for which your market gives you credit.
- **Align yourself with broad institutional goals.** The more you can demonstrate that branding can help the institution achieve its BHAG (big hairy audacious goals) agenda, the more likely you are to get broad-based support for the branding initiative.
- **Accept responsibility.** Indeed, welcome it.

- **Invite accountability,** as long as a reasonable level of authority comes with it.

- **Build networks,** both official and unofficial. You'll soon know who in your institution welcomes the impact and understands the process of a well-designed and implemented marketing initiative. Surprise them with coffee in the morning and take them for a glass of wine in the evening. Make sure they are prepared to successfully carry the branding flag forward.

- **Provide all necessary materials** and reports to keep the process moving.

- **Keep volunteer leadership in the loop** without letting them micromanage the process. Many members of your board will have had extensive experience with branding or brand marketing initiatives in the private sector. They can be strong allies, once they understand the differences in scale under which educational institutions operate. If they are accustomed to eight-figure advertising budgets, for example, they must be brought down gently about your institution's capacity to move the needle through a traditional advertising buy.

- **Befriend the faculty** and link their interests with yours. An engaged and informed faculty can be your greatest asset in keeping a branding initiative moving forward. Faculty need to know that a strengthened brand has direct and sustaining benefit for them, helping to: ensure better classroom dynamics through the attraction and recruitment of bright, ambitious students; position them as experts in the media and in their discipline; provide a basis for faculty recruitment and successful attainment of sponsored research contracts; encourage alumni and other donors to endow chairs or support other programs; and upgrade the general opinion of the institution.

- **Collect budget data.** At comprehensive and research institutions in particular, marketing and communications expenditures are highly decentralized. Sometimes, simply centralizing the advertising spend can generate new "found revenue" in the form of better volume rates. At Georgia Tech, bringing the advertising budget for athletics, continuing education, special events, and other decentralized units into the central office created enough elbow room for the institute to hire a market researcher.

- **Create incentives for participation,** from lunch to starring roles at launch, from budget infusion to programmatic support, from visibility in brand activation materials to free brand collateral tchotchkes (air freshener or hot cup sleeve, anybody?).

- **Stay open to new ideas.** It's easy to get trapped in the "expert" role; but to get newly hatched ambassadors excited about the brand, give them latitude to express and extend the brand in their own area of responsibility. Your role, then, is to guide, not define.

- **Constantly evolve the plan.** Your branding initiative will create a new market awareness and competitive positioning, often bringing heretofore out-of-reach institutions into the fray. It may also open the possibility of new programs or a new way to frame current programs in a more market-ready fashion. As these new programs emerge and develop, or as the new competitors enter the mix, your brand activation plan must adapt to these new market realities. The best plans are dog-eared, coffee-stained, festooned with Post-Its of various colors, highlighted and underlined. They are living documents, not the graveyard where all your institutional ambitions lie buried.

- **Keep doing research.** You need to know where you've arrived, how you're changing perceptions, what new opportunities are available to you. Market research is the only way to keep fresh, and the greater revenue that your branding effort is creating should provide the foundation for keeping a market research line in the budget.

- **Buy copies of *The Real U*** for everybody on your brand team. CASE needs the money. I need the visibility. We all need a shared playbook.

PUTTING IT ALL TOGETHER

When John D. Haeger took the reins at Northern Arizona University in November 2001, he faced a series of daunting challenges. The university's previous president had quit abruptly following serious allegations regarding personal misconduct. Enrollment had been declining since 1995, triggering a succession of budget-cutting years because of the state's per capita funding model. Faculty salaries had been frozen, leading to significant levels of faculty discontent. The physical plant suffered from severe deferred maintenance issues, and new facilities had long been on hold. The Arizona Board of Regents (ABOR), which supervises all three public universities in the state, was working on a plan to better define the roles of each institution, and alumni were disengaged.

Welcome aboard, Mr. President.

With ABOR support strong for the university as it redoubled its efforts to provide high-quality learning opportunities on the Flagstaff campus, at 37 physical sites statewide, and through a robust online capacity, Haeger led a strategic planning process that refocused the institution on its education mission and helped highlight its unique role in the Arizona higher ed marketplace. The university community rallied around the planning process and identified a number of graduate and professional programs that remained crucial to the institution's ability to fulfill its mission—even in a context in which serving the undergraduate population was seen as the "prime directive." Then through an integrated marketing committee led by Executive Vice President M. J. McMahon and Director of University Marketing Carla Andrews-O'Hara, an RFP was issued in 2003 for a firm to conduct market research, create a new verbal and visual identity system, and develop a comprehensive marketing plan for the university. Lipman Hearne was successful in our approach and began work in early 2004.

As we conducted our early interviews, we encountered a lot of folklore:

"You can't show snow in the recruitment materials, because that will scare off our prospects."
Yet many students were attracted to the university because it did offer something different from its competitors in the valley 6,000 feet below.

"People only go to NAU if they couldn't get in to UA or ASU."
Yet both qualitative and quantitative research would subsequently show that for four out of 10 students and alumni, Northern Arizona University was their first choice.

"Things just won't change."
Yet through President Haeger's efforts, a significant renewal was already under way.

Initial research consisted of both qualitative and quantitative inquiry—from one-on-one interviews to focus groups to Web-based and telephone surveys—that reached more than 4,000 stakeholders in the institution: administrators, faculty, staff, alumni, current students (undergraduate and graduate), prospective students and their parents, ABOR representatives, community leaders, and high school teachers and counselors. From this work, a number of key findings emerged:

- Faculty exhibited strong commitment to undergraduate education.
- The competitive environment was relatively clear-cut—but prospective students could distinguish between key aspects of NAU's "offer" and those of its competitors only in limited ways.
- Location was an essential part of institutional identity.
- Academic quality was not receiving sufficient attention in marketing materials.
- Disjointed marketing efforts were preventing the university from meeting its goals.
- Alumni were proud of their degree but didn't feel it was respected by their employers and peers.

We moved forward then on two fronts: developing a new institutional identity to replace the old, chaotic, and widely mutated version, and developing a new institutional positioning and integrated marketing plan.

This new identity, with mountain and tree symbols enclosed in a classic heraldic shield (see below) suggests both place and academic intent, with cool colors that contrast with the more strident tones used by the university's competitors. Moreover, in contrast to the previous institutional identity, this mark can be used effectively in all formats, including Web-based banner ads and Flash presentations. A program to launch the identity internally met with great enthusiasm, providing focus and energy to the more nuanced brand messaging process that lay ahead.

The positioning platform took into account the stature, size, and focus of the institution's competitors for mind- and market-share: the major research universities in the Valley of the Sun. The positioning was straightforward: Northern Arizona University offers "The Difference that Matters."

It matters that ...
- we balance teaching, scholarship, and service.
- we are committed to lifelong learning.
- we meet all students where they are and take them where they want to go.
- we provide an alternative to the sun-baked mega-campuses elsewhere in the state.
- we provide access to education and career preparation for students from all walks of life.
- we have a clear vision of our future and a sense of new ways to achieve that vision.
- we live in a community that values our presence.

These "differentiators" then led to a key creative insight: Students who choose to attend Northern Arizona University have made a positive, deliberate choice to take "the road less traveled." NAU students are proud of being contrary, are confident in their own, out-of-the-ordinary choices. It's not just location as *place*, it's location as an indicator of individual character. And from that insight sprang the "door-opener" campaign. With a very limited ad buy, we'd have to surprise the market, get people talking. And conventional "attribute" presentation just wouldn't work. So we devised a campaign based around four challenging statements:

- Mountain air makes you smarter.
- Get a 7,000-foot head start on life.
- Learn how to move mountains.
- Sea level is for wimps.

Market testing confirmed that prospective students, current students, and alumni all loved this bold, cheeky approach—though institutional leadership (wisely, thinking about ABOR members and other influencers who lived in the valley) decided it wasn't wise to roil the waters by calling anybody a wimp. And so a campaign was launched, including print, out-of-home (billboard and mallscape), digital, and viral elements.

The campaign was a huge success, exciting both comment and controversy as soon as it hit the streets. Faculty at NAU and competing institutions engaged in mock serious discussions about the quality of mountain air: "It's the ozone!" "It's the purity!" Alumni were challenged: "Does mountain air really make you smarter?" Newspapers covered the launch of the campaign and opined about its claims. National magazines picked up the campaign and attached it to stories about vacationing in Flagstaff. And everybody—even those with tongue firmly in cheek—had a distinctive point of pride. Students had a "badge" to which they could attach their choice. Alumni had a stance that contrasted with the old assumption: You didn't get into ASU. Faculty had a bit of a *frisson* from being associated with an institution that was making an assertive, sophisticated, humorous statement.

The Successful Identity Launch

Start at the beginning. Don't wait until the brand is developed to decide how to roll out or implement an identity. As soon as you start planning a new branding initiative, find and enlist internal champions. One of the biggest mistakes I've seen is that sometimes institutions are so busy looking at external audiences and market trends that they forget about their internal constituencies.

These internal champions provide valuable insights into institutional strengths and weaknesses, open possible channels of opportunity, and often offer strong suggestions on ways to carry the message forward. But more important, they also have valuable resources to help integrate the brand throughout the institution both in terms of staff and resources. As a result, their involvement helps the brand evolve naturally—almost organically—through each unit.

The amount of detail involved in rolling out an identity can be overwhelming. There are the obvious things like image and directional signage, stationery, banners and flags, and recruitment materials, but there are other, less obvious things that can be a challenge. Some of those include printed checks, classroom lecterns, athletic uniforms, rubber stamps used in the mail room, and cups in the dining halls, to name just a few. By working with a diverse internal constituency, you can identify these items and make sure to

include them in a brand integration plan. Drawing on information from the internal audience across campus will help you better focus your energy, resources, and budgets.

The sooner these materials are developed, the sooner channels of engagement blossom and the new identity is accepted in the marketplace— hence that natural, organic growth. But what about variants and alternate identities? How can you overcome the "we're different" perspective of some units? As a marketing professional, you can certainly acknowledge and even celebrate those internal differences as they contribute to the foundational, function, and emotional identity of the institution.

Yet, the overarching brand platform does not change. The brand is the very essence (or core) of the institution, and a strong brand makes fluidity in sub-branding possible. For example, Northern Arizona University positions itself as a different kind of institution in Arizona. It promotes a "difference that matters." The core of the identity is in its difference. The brand platform pushes what's different and why. Each unit embraces "the difference that matters" message and adapts it to its target audience or constituency. The university's Distance Learning Extended Campuses unit offers a good example of this sub-branding. Northern Arizona University has a large nontraditional student population scattered throughout Arizona and the region. The Extended Campuses unit has its own marketing department but has integrated "the difference that matters" message into its marketing efforts by also adopting the "We're everywhere you want to learn" message to support the institutional claim of difference.

The Distance Learning Extended Campuses unit is different because it has campuses throughout the state, because it has more than 80 online programs, and because the student population is older, working, and part-time. However, core institutional attributes identified in the brand platform, like personalized attention and small classes, are the same, and the nontraditional student population shares the same brand experience as the traditional student population. These different populations then share their experience with others in their circle of influence for a kind of organic realization across multiple channels. By the way, Northern Arizona University has seen extraordinary enrollment growth since beginning its branding initiative and

is now also enjoying increased awareness and outcomes from other constituency groups like alumni and donors.

So start with outcomes in mind and be sure to include internal expertise. This approach may take a bit longer, but it's well worth the effort. Build a branding initiative and brand activation plan that addresses short- and long-term goals. Include training and resources to help educate all on-campus audiences about the brand. Establish a marketing fund and share your budget with others. You'll be amazed how much good will a small investment can make. Drill down and remember the details. They always make a difference.

Although you will face your share of challenges (and occasionally beat your head against the wall), building a brand is an exciting time. So remember to have a little fun. Laughter goes a long way in building a brand—and in building relationships.

Carla Andrews-O'Hara
CAO Consulting

And so we moved into the next phase of the campaign: reinforcing "the difference that matters" by emphasizing the benefits of key differentiating aspects of NAU, including faculty as mentors, student-centered experience, and personal attention. This campaign continued into 2009 and, as a second wave of research proved, was remarkably successful.

Student-centered

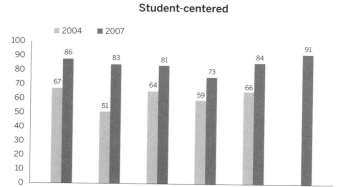

Personal

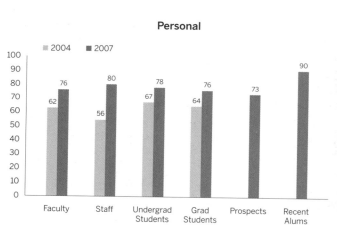

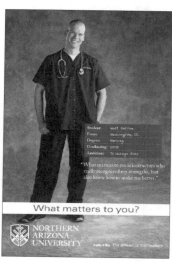

Perhaps the most important measure of the success of this campaign is that all stakeholder groups—those who deliver and experience the brand and those who anticipate what they will receive from it—rallied around the key attributes in a way that demonstrated their authenticity. When both faculty and students see faculty as mentors, mentoring happens. When undergrads and graduate students, faculty and staff, prospects and alumni, all see the institution as being student-centered and personal, those pledges are being kept. And with greater understanding of NAU's unique offer, and the institutional ability to deliver on its brand promise, came the desired results: a nearly decade-long downward trend in enrollment dramatically reversed—and continues to climb.

Increasing enrollment

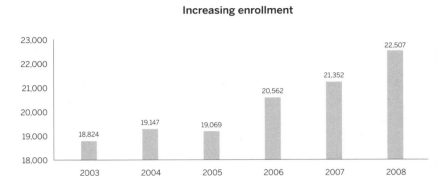

As any good marketer would ask: Was there a correlation between the increased investment in marketing and their results? And, of course (since I wouldn't have asked the question if I couldn't answer it), the answer is "yes."

Increasing enrollment

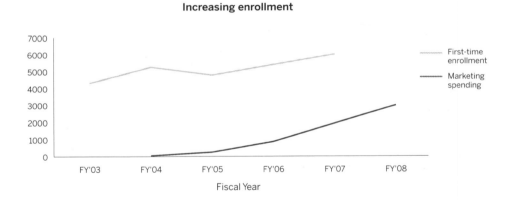

Another factor here, however, is the work of the enrollment management team itself. At Northern Arizona University, recruitment staff led by Vice President David Bousquet and Associate Vice President Jeannette Baker developed a remarkably effective prospect management system coordinated with the overall marketing campaign. The banner ads, billboards, and keyword purchases were instrumental in softening the market and cultivating greater understanding of the university's unique positioning, but it was up to the enrollment team to close the deal, which they did with style and energy.

No campaign like this succeeds without a great team, and throughout the ranks at Northern Arizona University, faculty and staff enthusiastically got on board with an exciting and effective integrated marketing campaign, thereby strengthening the brand immeasurably.

Campaigns such as these are successful because of effective process, insightful market research, smart positioning, great creative—and loads of determination. And they can have other surprising benefits. In large part because of the way the institution was positioned, Northern Arizona University received its largest gift ever: a commitment of $25 million from William Franke, who wasn't an alumnus but had a deep appreciation for NAU's singular focus on undergraduate education. And while a branding campaign can't necessarily guarantee eight-figure gifts, it can play a role in successful capital campaign initiatives.

For details, read on.

1. Jayne Merkel, "Cincinnati: Capital of the Avant-garde," *Cincinnati Magazine* 32 (November 1998): 75.

CHAPTER 9

CAMPAIGN BRANDING

BRANDING CAMPAIGNS are typically driven by enrollment goals—not surprisingly, since enrollment revenues are so critically important to colleges and universities nationwide and since a new crop of first-year students must be harvested every year. But major capital campaigns also offer an institution a terrific opportunity to define, position, and enhance its brand in another critical marketplace: that of alumni, donors, friends, and prospects who will make the gifts that allow the institution it achieve its broader strategic goals.

Think about it: Most years, the great majority of institutional communications resources are focused on enrollment-oriented outreach—print, Web, advertising, direct marketing. But in the year of a gala campaign kickoff, advancement marketing—campaign branding—often predominates.

CAMPAIGN BRANDING PROCESS

The process of developing a campaign brand begins with a feasibility study. As with any other branding initiative, the imperative is to find out from the target audience—in this case, rich folks—how they regard the institution itself, how they relate to the brand. Formally, and in most circumstances, this study is conducted by fundraising counsel, but occasionally there's a more limited and informal testing-the-waters period administered by institutional staff. All feasibility studies are built to assess the depth and readiness of the donor community to step up to the campaign challenge; a good marketing-oriented feasibility study also probes image, reputation, perception, and awareness issues that will be important in developing a strong and compelling campaign brand. If the feasibility study indicates that a campaign is likely to be successful—which almost all of them do, even if the goal is lowered and the specific objectives refocused—the institution goes into the quiet phase of the campaign, in which key donors (including board members and committed friends) are solicited for nucleus or principal gifts. At this time, the campaign brand is also developed.

When working to understand and articulate a campaign brand, I believe in a proven process:

- Review all primary materials.
  > Print pieces directed at advancement audiences, such as annual reports and annual fund solicitation materials
  > Feasibility study report, including prospectus provided to interview respondents and notes from interviews (if available)
  > Alumni magazine and publications from key schools and colleges
  > President/chancellor speeches
  > Recruitment and enrollment materials
  > Primary Web pages
  > ASQ, NSSE, and other relevant data
  > Market research data, particularly alumni surveys or focus group findings
  > Brand or identity manuals
- Interview key "voices."
  > President/chancellor
  > Deans of key colleges
  > Board chair
  > Campaign chair
  > Selected board members, focusing on those who are regarded as key "influentials" or those with marketing or communications expertise
  > Chief development officer
  > Major gift officers
  > Chief communications officer
  > Communications staff members
- Review competitor materials, knowing that *philanthropic* competitors cover a broader range than enrollment competitors; in any given environment, the symphony orchestra, art museum, hospital, or issue-based organization might be a major player in the mind of the marketplace.
- Develop campaign communicator's kit.
  > Insider's case statement (if necessary)
  > Campaign communications plan, including key messages, recommended materials, timeline for production
- Develop campaign brand alternatives, including theme, identity, and primary applications.
- Present alternatives to staff/board committee.
- Select, refine, apply campaign brand to primary materials.
  > Identity system
  > Pocket folder

> Primary and secondary brochures
> Proposal cover
> Pledge card
> Web site or giving microsite
> PowerPoint
> Video/DVD

• Produce materials.

In this work, there is frequently a "matrix of responsibility" between institutional staff and campaign communications counsel, with the former providing key insights and instincts about the institution and its supporters and the latter providing perspective, experience, and a singular ability to get the job done on time and under pressure.

Your Annual Giving Brand

I've visited many schools, colleges, and universities where the fundraising staff helpfully took the time to brief me that "our alumni love this place, they just don't choose to express it through their giving."

It's not their fault if you haven't developed an annual giving culture and brand for your institution. An annual giving brand can help connect the dots in the minds of constituents—the connection between affinity for your institution and *expressing* that affinity through giving.

People look at institutions with long-established traditions of giving (longer than theirs, anyway) and presume that the culture has always existed. They fail to give credit for the strong annual giving brands that exist at those schools. This failure is not as much a factor of the institution's history as much as the successful history of its annual giving brand.

I often use the analogy of a crowd doing "the wave" at a sporting event. You know the wave—the glorious group exercise where seating sections stand up in sequence and create the effect of a wave undulating around a stadium. Before the crazy student section decides to start the wave, everyone's perfectly happy watching the game. Yet within just a few minutes, everyone's paying attention to the wave and their participation in it.

The wave forces you to quickly think about a few things. It teaches you what you're supposed to do—stand up at the right time. It also causes you to think about the implications of not standing up: "What's the matter with that guy?"

We're trying to accomplish the same thing in annual giving, and it's OK to accept that most people weren't thinking about supporting us before we showed up.

Institutions often lose two-thirds of their first-time donors the following year. Your annual giving brand is perhaps most important when thinking about the *annual* in annual giving. These are the facets of your annual giving brand:

• The consistent and recurring way with which you **articulate your case for support**. People connect with consistent and compelling annual giving motivations. These include differentiating between annual gifts and other types of gift support for your institution.

• Your ability to **demonstrate a culture of constituent participation** (from peer advocates and others in the community). Annual giving is often about a celebration of community members raising their hands and making a statement of support.

• Your effectiveness at **stewarding and cultivating a relationship with your donors**. Annual giving isn't just about solicitations, it's about the whole experience a donor has as a supporter; how well you say thanks, how well you keep donors informed, and how much better they feel when they support you instead of other organizations.

If your constituents don't connect their good feelings with gift support, it's not their fault. They're suffering from your lack of an annual giving brand.

Bob Burdenski
Principal
Robert Burdenski Annual Giving

CAMPAIGN BRANDS IN CONTEXT

In all this work, one principle needs to stay paramount: People don't give to the *campaign*, they give to the *institution*. Therefore, the institutional brand—how people feel about it, how they perceive it, how they define its role, how they understand its relevance to their concerns—remains the primary lodestone for the campaign brand. But the institutional brand, by itself, is not enough to energize a campaign brand. Campaign brands must both resonate with and challenge institutional brands, since nobody gives mega-gifts to sustain the status quo. Campaign branding must push beyond the immediate value proposition into the potential impact of the institution after it has achieved its campaign goals, all the while still passing the "sniff test" for those people who know and love the institution.

Campaign brands are developed in the context of institutional character and specific campaign objectives. Endowment campaigns, for example, would require a far more people-focused brand than would campaigns that were primarily to support capital improvements or program development. All campaigns, though, have to answer three fundamental questions:

1. Why this institution?

2. Why these projects?

3. Why now?

The first question is answered through institutional and campaign branding; the others are answered through the development of effective, segmented campaign branding collateral.

Perhaps the most effective way to explain how this dynamic plays out is through case studies. An exploration of four different campaign branding narratives—for the University of Miami, University of Wisconsin–Milwaukee, Brown University, and Denison University—will illustrate a number of different challenges and effective campaign branding solutions.

The University of Miami

The University of Miami shares a name, and to some extent a brand, with one of the most evocative locales in the United States. Miami: sun, speed, South Beach, style, fashionistas. Moreover, the university has, in recent decades, become a true "player" in South Florida, largely through the impact of its medical school, though public understanding of and appreciation for this role paled in comparison to Hurricane football fever. The university had been gaining in strength and reputation for a number of years, a process that greatly accelerated when Donna Shalala became president in 2001. President Shalala is, herself, a human hurricane: a force of nature that blows through obstacles without pause. Soon after she assumed the reins at the university, Shalala announced her intention to launch a $1 billion capital campaign, an ambitious increase on the institution's previous fundraising initiatives.

A campaign theme, "Momentum: The Campaign for the University of Miami," was developed to reflect the dynamism of the university and the relentless energy of its president. Momentum captures all that is relevant about the university and the campaign:

- We're an institution on the move, rising rapidly in stature and impact.
- We're not content with the status quo.
- We're not to be stopped.
- We're going to get there—with your help.

To express the brand, an identity mark was developed that was drawn from a core element of the university's seal: a stylized sun with rays made of interlocking *M*s. It was executed as an embossed holographic metal foil, hand-tipped onto the covers of the print materials. Obviously, a holographic metal foil identity wouldn't be appropriate for Mother Hubbard's School for Shy Girls, but for the University of Miami it sent all the right signals: top quality, assertive, bold, proud. And the materials that supported the campaign furthered the brand agenda. They are dramatic, surprising, oversized statements of institutional stature, energy, and unstoppable momentum. The video that was developed for the gala launch of the campaign further advanced the brand expression. Full of music, quick cuts, and multiple overlapping storylines, it features the work of a dozen camera crews—some of them students—all of whom shot activities at the university in one hour one September morning. Called *Miami in an Hour*, it is actually six minutes of incredibly compressed energy. The splash page on the Web started with a Flash animation of the campaign logo and featured a number of active and interactive features.

M O M E N T U M

THE CAMPAIGN FOR THE

UNIVERSITY OF MIAMI

The print materials accentuated the close connection of the university and the city, making *Miami* and *Momentum* synonymous with the university. The brand claim is clearly stated: "Great cities need great institutions," and the materials position the university as a key contributor to the stature, growth, and future of the city and region.

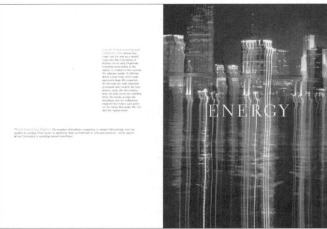

The campaign was a success on all fronts, raising nearly $1.4 billion and clearly positioning the university as a "player" in the south Florida philanthropic landscape. Moreover, the energy of the branded campaign materials helped create an infectious sense of opportunity and excitement on campus and in the broader community.

University of Wisconsin–Milwaukee

When you say "University of Wisconsin" almost anywhere in the Midwest, the great majority of people assume you're talking about the flagship in Madison. And why not? The Badgers are in the Big Ten and therefore consistently on television in major markets throughout the nation; the institution was founded before the Civil War; it enrolls more than 40,000 students and has graduated nearly 400,000 alumni, including Dick Cheney, Charles Lindbergh, Joyce Carol Oates, and Frank Lloyd Wright.

But UW–Madison's urban sister in Milwaukee boasts a full array of undergraduate, graduate, and professional programs; enrolls nearly 24,000 undergraduate students annually; and has long demonstrated a profound and lasting impact on the economic and social fabric of southeast Wisconsin, the population center of the state. When Carlos E. Santiago became chancellor of the University of Wisconsin–Milwaukee in 2004, he immediately launched an effort to enhance and solidify the university's role and reputation that quickly won support from civic and business leaders—so much so that focus groups conducted among these leaders in 2006 found them quoting Chancellor Santiago about UWM's mission. Based on market research and an institutional positioning process, a theme emerged—"Something Great in Mind"—that became the driver for both the institutional branding effort and the capital campaign. Print, radio, out-of-home, and Web executions were developed to build awareness of outstanding UWM people and their contributions to the economic vitality of the region. If you Google "Something Great in Mind" you'll be led directly to the UW–Milwaukee Web site.

As planning went forward for a new and ambitious revenue initiative—targeting $100 million in private support, $100 million in increased support from the state, and $100 million in additional federal research contracts—creative execution pivoted off this same concept. For one-on-one donor cultivation and solicitation, print materials were developed using the same set of profiles, exemplifying the kind of impact that a donor could achieve through an investment in UWM. The campaign exceeded its goal after a public launch in August 2006, successfully "slipstreaming" on the positioning and energy of the branding initiative to raise $125 million a year before its anticipated close.

Brown University

Brown University alumni have at times labored to take pride in the university's distinction, its defining differences. A "founding Ivy," Brown shares many of the characteristic brand features of its sister institutions: top-flight faculty, great students, international reputation, significant research contributions, stellar alumni, and the like. But Brown is different. With its adoption of the open curriculum four decades ago, Brown created a distinct differentiation for itself and left itself open to the charge that it was not as serious or as rigorous as its peers. Brown people, profoundly, feel differently. They want Brown to be respected and admired by its peers, to compete successfully for the best students and faculty, to make research contributions on a par with the top institutions in the world. They want the open curriculum—in which highly talented students create their own path to knowledge assimilation and synthesis—to be respected for its own idiosyncratic rigor and challenge. They want Brown to be more highly regarded. But they don't want Brown to become "not Brown" in the process.

Branding Brown

When Brown University began the process of developing materials needed for the public launch of our campaign in 2005, we had everything in place: the campaign goals, the campaign priorities, the campaign leadership ... everything, that is, except the campaign name. What we needed was a short, hard-working tagline that would say something essential about the campaign, fire up our volunteers and alumni, and—would it be too much to ask?— capture the unique nature of Brown as an educational institution.

The campaign was ambitious: a $1.4 billion goal for the smallest university in the Ivy League, and one with a modest record of fundraising success. The new president was an inspiring, vigorous leader who was not just planning for momentous change, but implementing it by hiring dozens of new faculty, initiating new programs, launching need-blind admission. Her confidence in the future inspired a new level of ambition on campus that was matched by a sense of excitement among the volunteer leadership. What was the tagline that would succinctly express all this ambition, vision, momentum, urgency, courage, and pride—and keep inspiring it?

Though we had grown used to it, our consultants remarked that it was not unusual to hear the word Brown used as an adjective. "That is so Brown!" someone would say—of a student with a triple major in, say, computer science, philosophy, and Greek. Or of the undergraduate curriculum that offers more than 100 concentrations because our entrepreneurial students are known for their intellectual initiative. Or of a pioneering research project in which undergraduates are valued partners—and occasionally emerge as first authors. Or of an administration that began implementing the ambitious Plan for Academic Enrichment in advance of the campaign designed to support it. "That is so Brown!"

Can an adverb modify a noun? It can when that noun is also an adjective, when that noun is Brown. With "Boldly Brown," the Campaign for Academic Enrichment got the tagline it needed to express the distinctive qualities, not just of the campaign, but of the university itself. And when the students began wearing T-shirts that said "not timid," we knew we had gotten it right.

Susan Weston
Director of Development Communications and Stewardship
Brown University

Ruth Simmons, president of Brown, strongly believed that the $1.4 billion Brown initiative had to be framed as "The Campaign for Academic Enrichment" because she saw it as providing extraordinary funds for core academic purposes: hiring great faculty, recruiting undergraduate students, creating stipends and fellowships for graduate students in key areas, building new science and research facilities. A pragmatist to the core, President Simmons wanted the campaign to reinforce the essentials rather than launch new and different initiatives. She saw it as an opportunity to apply the fundamental Brown undergraduate experience of cross-disciplinary and syncretic thinking to the graduate and professional education that had traditionally been more discipline-specific. And while alumni donors, in particular, were excited by the president's vision, they were also concerned that the shift toward emphasizing graduate and professional schools would in some way erode the quality or character of Brown's undergraduate experience.

The solution was to wrap the fundraising initiative in a clarion call to the whole university community by framing it as "Boldly Brown: The Campaign for Academic Enrichment." With the "Boldly Brown" campaign theme, alumni and loyalists could rally around their pride and distinction while still contributing to the academic essentials that President Simmons saw as central to the future success of the institution. "Boldly Brown" played out in a number of ways. A dramatic print piece used a variety of visual and photographic styles and production techniques to express the unique and dialogic nature of the Brown experience. In the judges' comments that accompanied the CASE Grand Gold that was awarded to the Brown materials, they noted "everything about this package feels intentional ... outstanding photos, compelling quotes, strong concept—all made the case statement a very well-resolved communications piece. But the essential, most important quality was the perceived authenticity of the writing. The case statement had Brown's voice."

The campaign video took a similar route, shooting student and faculty representatives in a variety of settings and clothing choices. As each person spoke, the background and look changed to reflect the multidisciplinary, interactive nature of the Brown experience. And the student body gladly took up the "Boldly Brown" mantra, producing T-shirts that boasted "Not Timid" and in other ways celebrating their pride in being part of the Brown mystique.

Moreover, the campaign gave the university the means to express the many different ways that Brown acts—dynamically, uniquely, expressively, philanthropically. And linking an adverb with a proper noun boldly turns that proper noun into—nearly—a verb. So "to Brown" becomes an energetic, affirmative way of being. The campaign not only exceeded its $1.4 billion goal, it reaffirmed and reenergized the Brown brand, making alumni, students, and other stakeholders true brand ambassadors.

Denison University

At Denison University, a campaign goal of $160 million was focused on endowment for people and programs, enabling Denison to continue to compete successfully with other small, elite colleges and universities for top students and high-achieving faculty. As an undergraduate, liberal arts institution, Denison has long built its brand on the whole student experience, anchored by an academic focus on intellectual exploration, faculty-guided research, small classes, and strong personal advising. But when alumni and parents of students and alumni were asked what really stood out for them about Denison, what anchored their perception and sparked their passion, they always referred to two elements: *people* and *place.*

Denison's campus is stretched along a "backbone" ridge above the town of Granville, Ohio. Rather than presenting a classic square campus quad framed by redbrick buildings, Denison's village green follows the ridgeline, offering both a sense of enclosure from the brick and limestone Georgian Revival buildings, as well as surprising vistas between the buildings to the town and countryside below. This visual cue—along with students' memories of trudging back up the steep hill to campus from a visit to Granville—provided the basis for the campaign theme: "Higher Ground: The Campaign for Denison."

"Higher Ground" works on many levels. First, it reinforces one of the primary Denison attributes: a sense of aerie, a remembrance of that separate, special place where alumni spent their formative years. It also expresses an aspiration for the institution: We are not content with the status quo but are taking Denison to new heights. And finally, it positions the campaign as the driver of those aspirations: With your help, we will fulfill our promise, rise to new heights, achieve the prominence you and we know we deserve. Key messages supported the central claim, building around concepts such as higher standards, higher expectations, and higher aspirations.

The campaign was launched with an on-campus gala followed by a series of regional events. Print materials, video, and Web expression of the brand were accompanied by a treasure trove of "Higher Ground" tchotchkes: ball caps, golf towels, cup holders, beach towels, mouse pads, and the like, all of which were eagerly snapped up by the alumni, donors, and friends who attended the events. Even more important, supporters are responding with their checkbooks, estate plans, and appreciated assets. The campaign exceeded its $160 million goal by more than 10 percent when it closed.

WHAT PRICE SUCCESS?

Years ago, we would hear from college and university administrators that "our donors don't want to see materials that look like they cost a lot of money." We don't hear that concern as much anymore. This doesn't mean that cost is no object, or that donor sensitivities to cost and perceived "lavish" materials are not important, but it does mean that there's a greater understanding now of the competitive context in which campaign materials operate.

First, the quality of branded materials that support campaign initiatives has risen dramatically over the past five to 10 years: Donor expectations have been raised. Next, as the saying goes, "you only have one chance to make a good first impression"—and in the media-saturated, rapid-decision environment in which we now live, that impression has to be strong, evocative, and on-target if the development office is to keep the door open. Finally, the standards for the materials are being set by their primary target audience: the mega- and major-gift donors who are committing seven- and eight-figure gifts to the institution. And those donors are assessing the wisdom of that investment with the same brain they use to consider other multimillion-dollar decisions, so the competitive context includes fancy business plans from IPOs, financial planning documents from Fidelity, annual reports from Fortune 100 companies, and the prospectus for Donald Trump's latest penthouse extravaganza.

Should campaign materials be "slick"? In most cases, probably not; but the perception of slickness can be addressed through uncoated paper stocks and other modifiers of the tactile experience, without any reduction in important production values. Should they be smart? Should they have clarity, impact, energy, life? Darn tootin'. Otherwise they'll just get lost in the shuffle and not advance the kind of donor engagement with the future that characterizes successful campaigns.

Nobody makes a mega-gift decision based on the quality of the materials. Far more important is the donor's ability to give and his or her interest in the institution, the sincerity and dedication of institutional leadership and development staff, the "read" that staff has made of the donor's interests. But the quality of the materials can significantly buttress the institutional case, reassure the donor that the institution has its act together, and act as a focus of donor pride both before and after the gift has been made. Major gifts are the result of real belief and engagement, of commitment to and belief in the institution. They are a confirmation of the relevance and power of the brand.

CONCLUSION AND PARTING WORDS

IN A RECENT PRESENTATION, an advertising executive made the case: "Brands command higher prices." So that's why we do it. Even though, in higher ed, it's not only a higher price that we want to command. We want more enthusiasm, greater loyalty, undying affection, and, yes, love. We want prospects to flock to us, students to persist and succeed, parents to gladly write those checks, alumni to bleed our school colors when scratched, faculty to hurl themselves body and soul into the development and transmission of intellectual excitement, neighbors to appreciate our very presence, corporate and foundation reps to say "yes" to whatever we ask of them, and administrators to open the budget coffers because they recognize positive return on investment when they see it.

Brands are about big ideas—resonant concepts that strike home and find a place in our lives. We return to them again and again because they satisfy a need, scratch an itch, fulfill a dream. And higher ed brands become part and parcel of the stories that we tell about ourselves, that inform the larger narrative of how we came to be who we are, who we're still becoming. I couldn't understand or articulate who I am without some reference to my undergraduate institution (University of California at Santa Cruz, where I survived the Sixties and met my first wife—whom I almost didn't survive), the institution where I got my master's (University of Idaho, where I found an institutional home after a decade on the freelance writing circuit), or doctoral institution (University of Illinois at Chicago, where I met my *real* wife, learned the language of literary criticism with which I can still occasionally pass as an academic, and got a toehold in a big new city that in the end became my home). In my life, these higher ed brands play a big role, and they have an underlying, mission-based story. They are all public institutions, because without state-supported systems a Navy brat like me couldn't have hoped to go to college, much less eventually arrive at a Ph.D. They are each a place in time, and my time in a place, in which I found friends, learned things, and made decisions that propelled me farther down the road to "me." Some of this progress took place in the classroom, and a lot of it took place in residence halls, apartments, homes, basketball or squash courts, cafés, and roadside attractions in which I worked or idled along the way.

None of this is unique. My particular version has its own tint, of course, but we all have a personal brand story, informed in large part by those places we lived and learned in our life journey. *Alma mater* is not a misnomer. We are made as much by our educational touchstones as we are by the family that raised us. For each of us, the story of our life is a story of learning, of becoming, of the choices we made that led us where we are. And what each institution wants from its branding initiative is for us as stakeholders to feel even greater affiliation with the institution where we chose to matriculate—where people are making that very same choice today. Institutions want us to know the Real U, and to love it.

Early in my career as a writer—three unpublished novels (one with an actual ISBN before the publisher went under), numerous stories and poems in magazines large and small, fourth- and fifth-grade grammar and social studies textbooks—I would have been surprised to learn that I'd be writing one day about branding in higher education. Even my doctoral work was focused on determining the elements of the Great American Novel—which I contend hasn't been written yet, because I haven't had the time to do so. (Writers are nothing if not arrogant.) But brands might well be the Great American Narrative, linking personal choice and identity with the social engine of capitalism. If we are what we buy or what we consume—or if those choices signal our own beliefs and proclamations about self—what could be more American than a brand?

Your own Real U brand—your alma mater—reflects who you are in meaningful ways. You own it; it owns you. Do you wear your university's hoodie proudly as you shovel snow or the workout T as you sweat on the elliptical, or do you don somebody else's brand? And why? And can you take this understanding of how you relate to your own alma mater brand to find a way to express the Real U for the institution you serve? Because that Real U needs you—your skills, your intelligence, your experience, your passion.

If your Real U is to succeed in the world, it needs the full impact of the real you.

SUBJECT INDEX

Specific commercial brands mentioned in this text are listed under "commercial brands." Specific institutions of higher education may be found in the separate Index of Colleges and Universities.

INDEX OF COLLEGES AND UNIVERSITIES

ABOUT THE AUTHOR

ROBERT M. MOORE, Ph.D.
Managing Partner, Lipman Hearne

ROB MOORE has more than 25 years of experience providing marketing communications counsel and creative services for nonprofit organizations. Known nationally for his role in advancing the understanding and validity of effective marketing practices in higher education, Rob is a frequent presenter at national conferences and a leading contributor to industry periodicals, including CURRENTS, *Change*, and *Trusteeship*. Rob also launched and supervised the nation's first and only survey of marketing practices in higher education.

Rob's education clients have included Brown University, Bryant University, Culver Academies, Denison University, Duke University, Georgia Institute of Technology, Grand Valley State University, Harvey Mudd College, McDaniel College, Northern Arizona University, Sewanee—The University of the South, Seton Hall University, Sidwell Friends School, The College of New Jersey, Trinity University, UNITECH South Africa, University of Arizona Foundation, University of Birmingham (U.K.), University of California–San Francisco, University of California–Santa Cruz, University of Chicago, University of Illinois, University of Iowa, University of Miami, University of North Carolina at Chapel Hill, University of South Carolina, University of Sydney (Australia), University of Washington, University of Wisconsin–Stevens Point, and Wheaton College.

Rob holds a B.A. from University of California at Santa Cruz, an M.A. from the University of Idaho, and a Ph.D. in English from the University of Illinois at Chicago. He is a founding member of the CASE Industry Advisory Council, the Forum for Higher Education Marketing, and the Public Affairs Committee of Independent Sector.